Passionate Attention

Passionate Attention

An Introduction to Literary Study

RICHARD L. McGUIRE

W · W · NORTON & COMPANY · INC · New York

Contents

Preface

This book is primarily for students who are beginning their study of literature or who have decided that criticism's only function is to prove one reader right and another wrong. It is about the many ways rather than about "the one way" to study literary works. I wanted to write a book that would give readers and students of literature a comprehensive frame for their own particular interests and which would also help them to identify and assess the other approaches to literature that they encounter in classes, reading, and conversation.

The book starts by considering some questions often asked about literary study in the context of the values that I think are basic to that study. The rest of the text is devoted to examining the possibilities for expanding one's knowledge of a literary work after first meeting it on the page.

The phrase "passionate attention" is not my own; I have borrowed it from W. H. Auden's "Making, Knowing, and Judging," an essay which I rediscovered while writing this book. This book is the explanation of my use of Auden's phrase. I see the acts of living and of reading and studying literature as having value only if they are motivated by love and interest; "passionate attention" is thus the richest short description of literary criticism I know. It represents the two most important human qualities involved in a person's relationships with other persons and with literature. What I want to do in this book is to expand the possibilities of the act of literary inquiry so that the student of literature may see that criticism is an act that affirms the richness of the individual's own experience and mind.

I am indebted to all the persons whose names I mention or whose works I cite, as well as to all the students who led me to think about the subject. M. H. Abrams first taught me the richness of criticism through the beginning chapter of his book, *The Mirror and the Lamp*, where he sets out the four basic areas of experience which the study of literature is related to. I have continued to find his basic categories valuable and propose to use them in this book, but any mistaken applications of them are my own. The encouraging comments of Professor Abrams and J. Paul Hunter helped me to put the book in its final form. I also have immeasurable debts to John McCully, Carl Housman, Dennis Williams, and the late M. W. Askew.

Passionate Attention

CHAPTER ONE

The Twofold Process

My literary education is a hodgepodge. When I was in high school, it consisted of learning all the terminology of poetic devices (iambic pentameter, ode, sonnet, etc.) and reading plays and novels aloud in class. I read *Macbeth*, *Silas Marner*, and *A Tale of Two Cities*, and acted out *Our Town*, taking care not to step in the imaginary flower bed (for which I would have been banished to the back of the classroom).

My college undergraduate courses in English included a course in Shakespeare, in which we learned all about the "Bard's" deer-poaching and "enjoyed" Falstaff; a course in Chaucer, in which we were supposed to read him in the original; a course in the American novel, in which I read the books and in class sat in perpetual fear of the judgment of several graduate students encamped in the front row; and a course in the short story, for which I did a report on Ray Bradbury. There were other courses too (I needed thirty semester hours for a major) but I do not recall them. Looking back, I see that

I managed to stay ignorant of any education that trained me in literary "analysis." It was perhaps not a disaster that I remained so during that time, even though graduate school was consequently difficult for me. What I remember instead are a number of men who talked about the literature they loved in a variety of ways. Even though I didn't care a rap about Shakespeare's deer-poaching, I saw that Shakespeare's work delighted the man who talked about it. What I saw in the novel class was the intense interest of a man in the text of the work he was reading and teaching us about. I was a mediocre student, but I saw in his study of literature the intensity that I desired in my own.

My first stint of graduate school (for my M.A.) was more or less inconsequential except for the course I had in literary criticism. The man who taught that course was one who, according to today's vocabulary, "tore poems apart." But for me, he was putting them together anew. He was a "New Critic" and he was interested in "unity." It was from him that I discovered the mystery of the craft of the poet, for he showed me the way in which the various elements of the poem fit together. I now know that his technique would not have worked on all poems, and that it had its limitations. But the poems he chose to explicate were unified; consequently, he taught me how to read poems as I had never been able to before.

When I left with my M.A. (having learned by then how to read), I took a job at a small state university where I taught in much the same way that my criticism instructor had, and, as never before, I read deeply the works that I taught. That was preparation for going back to graduate school.

My second stint (for my Ph.D.) was my literary education, and it was then that I finally acquired the background of information about history, history of criticism, literary history, and mere names and dates, which now serve as the factual bases for my own critical inquiries. But what that information and several men taught me was that criticism was not simply the "New Criticism" and not simply an "objective approach." It was the personal relationship of a reader to the work in any of its many different aspects; the individuality of the reader was what made it valuable. It was about that time that I read M. H. Abrams's *The Mirror and the Lamp* and discovered that his treatment of kinds of criticism offered a way of seeing criticism in the light of its manifold possibilities.

But there is also one more event that stands in my mind as important to this personal history. It was not an encounter with a book or teacher, but it taught me about criticism. I saw a movie called *The Graduate*. The basic plot and theme is that a young man rejects the false values and hypocrisy of his social world and attempts to begin a new life for himself by running away with the girl he discovers he loves. The humor of the first part and the energy of the last part were captivating, and the story line was clear and coherent. I liked it. Thus I was surprised when I read a review of the movie and found that the reviewer thought it poorly done. The reviewer's complaint was that the film splits its tone; the first half of the film is satirical of all, including the young man who will become the hero; but the last half becomes serious about and sympathetic with the hero. Now if I accepted the criterion of the necessity for tonal unity, then I had to agree that the film was bad and that my first impression was mistaken. The reviewer's perception was correct; the film did change in tone. But did that lead to finding fault with the film? It occurred to me that the next question was not "Is it good or bad?" but "Why does it change in tone?" My answer was that it has to in order to make its point. As long as the hero is part of the society that is blatantly immoral, then he should be satirized. But when he moves out of that society, the film should show him as a better person and it does so by showing him in a more sympathetic light.

What I discovered in the course of my disagreement with

the critic was that we were both right, given our own criteria. He thought that the first demand was for consistency of tone and approach to the hero. I thought that the first demand was that the structure of the film support the message. We had each chosen a set of values we thought most important and had placed the film in the framework of those values. Looking back on my choice, I see now that there was yet another criterion underlying my supposedly literary one; I was willing to accept the fact that the young man could, by virtue of his growing sense of something wrong and by the sheer energy of his actions, break out of the immoral life he had been subjected to.

My experience of comparing judgments about the film, as I began to see its connection to the reading and study of literature, led me to the basic assumption of this book: *the reading and the study of literature cannot and do not take place outside the context of human values.* Unique personal experience, from which values come, is the stuff of which literature is made. Literature is not compounded out of the generalities of human experience or the consensus of a group. It is a record of specific personal perceptions. Herbert Read says that the artist "always confronts the unknown" and that that is an indication of the greatness of his vision; but he also says that the artist "brings back from that confrontation . . . a novelty, a new symbol, a new vision of life, the outer image of inward things." [1] What Read says of the task of the artist is also true of the critic, because each person must rediscover experience for himself, and bring it back to others. That which is valuable in the world is unique human experience which is offered in its richest semblance to another person, not that that person must accept it as law, but that his own vision may be enriched by having the vicarious vision of another person.

However, sometimes the task of bringing back one's own perceptions of literature is a difficult one to accept. The student may doubt that language serves in any way to establish relationships among persons. Consequently, the student may doubt the value of literature, too. The cause of this doubt may be his own uncertainty, even despair, of the value of his own unique personal experience. If a person decides that he is of no value, he will not see value in other persons or in literature. The source of his rejection of the experiences that art and the study of art can provide is the individual's disillusionment with himself as a source of intelligence and insight. Thus, when a teacher asks that student to express his own insight and opinions about a work, he may copy those of the teacher, read what a critic has said and copy that, or take refuge in the comment that everybody *feels* differently about what they read and there is no possibility of conveying that feeling to anybody else. What the student should realize is that the uniqueness of his responses and insights is precisely that which makes them valuable, because that is also the value in the literature he is reading. His attempt to convey these insights to others (which is literary criticism in its simplest form) is an affirmation of the richness of human experience that is reflected both in the work and its reader.

Criticism begins in the individual who is confident of his own capacities for seeing and hearing and responding. But it is not one's first immediate experience of literature. As Northrup Frye says: It is impossible to "learn literature," but one can learn about it,[2] and that is what criticism is. I said before that criticism is an act of love. We can never learn those people we love, but we can learn about them in such ways as to perceive more clearly that unfathomable, mysterious core that is the source of their beauty. The gathering of more and more knowledge (which is more than just information) enriches our own vision of that person. None of that knowledge defines or limits; it expands and makes more complete. It is true that knowledge can be used destructively, both on persons and on literature; that is why criticism is a moral act, like love. You must always choose how you are going to go about it.

So far, I have been talking about what criticism is for the student himself. The source of criticism in the individual affirms the uniqueness of a literary work and the response to it, and thus the infinite possibilities of individual variation in human life and creation. But the whole process of critical inquiry embraces the paradox of being human—that is, having a unique being, but also being a part of the community of mankind. Thus criticism must also be a social act; it must attempt to convey to others its own unique vision. Once you have asked yourself what about a work gives pleasure—the style, the form, the imagery, the ideas, the events behind it, what you discovered about the author, his time, or about the permanence of human values—then you must ask yourself how you can best reveal this interest and pleasure to someone else.

The twofold process of literary study is an act of faith. It is a statement of belief in the possibility that these peculiar marks which are called letters and words can somehow embody a person's experience in such a way as to make that experience available to another. Literature, whether it be fiction, poetry, critical, expository, or whatever, affirms the human community *and* the uniqueness of the individual. To deny this paradox is to deny the paradox of being human, of being common and unique in the same moment.

To be human is to affirm not only one's individuality but also one's *kind* and the possibility of community. Literature proves the richness, not the limitations of being human, and literary criticism is the activity that seeks continually to demonstrate the significance and profundity of the work in such a way that it is there for all people to see and take delight in.

One student said that he would feel better about literary study if it weren't called "criticism." The word has come to

have unpleasant connotations for students who enjoy literature. This is because it is associated with reductive and dogmatic statements which students have come to believe consti-
tute all criticism, not just bad criticism. When I suggested
that he substitute the word "illumination," he said that that
made such study seem valuable. However, though I do think
of criticism as illumination, I do not believe that we need the
substitute word. "Criticism" means not only to judge, but also
to "discern," and it is the latter definition that best defines the
process in all its aspects. (The judgmental aspect is only one
kind of criticism.) The ability to discern is the ability to see,
and that is the first act of the process. The critical process can
be described as the act of discerning followed by the act of
illumination. The first indicates the reader's relationship to
the work; the second, the reader-critic's relationship to his
audience.

"What approach should I take?"

The above question is a code sentence which students use in
talking to teachers of literature. The translation is: "What is
your own critical approach and how can I best make my work
conform to it?" There are two ways for teachers to respond
to this. Some will want the student to learn their own critical
biases, and if that is the case, their answer should be a forth-
right explanation of that wish. Other teachers will say, "I want
you to take your own approach." But this statement can mean
two things. The instructor may think of his class as an exercise
in finding the critical needle in the verbal haystack. In this
case, the teacher's sentence is also code. It means "I want you
to find out what my bias is, and find a new way of writing
about it." Woe to the student who does not know how to
interpret that code correctly! On the other hand, the teacher's

response may mean exactly what it says, that he wants the student to formulate his own criteria and to offer his interpretation of the work based on those criteria.

Unfortunately, just knowing that there is a code in some of these replies does not keep a student from being penalized for taking his own approach. The only thing that can be done when a teacher says that he wants the student to formulate his own approach is to do just that. But, you will say, what about the real concern; that is, what kind of grade will the student get for persisting in the approach that was supposedly given him? The issue is a moral one—what is more important, getting the grade or doing what one thinks is best? It's a choice the student makes and this book will not necessarily help him get better grades.

"I don't like to tear poems apart"

The statement above is another code sentence and it comes in various forms: "I don't like to dissect literature"; "I don't like to analyze poetry"; "You can't really discuss poems because they mean something different to each reader." All are variations on the same theme. The phrases "tearing poems apart" and "dissecting literature" are metaphors. They are not literally true, short of ripping a page out of an anthology or cutting up the text of the work. Whether the student really believes what he is saying is another question. Sometimes such phrases are clichés used as rationalizations for avoiding literary study. Other times, the statements are legitimate, even though metaphorical responses, and they come from intelligent, well-read people. Consequently, I have come to believe that these comments deserve consideration; otherwise literary criticism will continue to disappoint the students who respond to the works as though they have a life of their own which should not be destroyed.

Sometimes it is difficult for the student to realize that the practice of passing judgment on literary works is not a universally approved activity, because the commentary he most often encounters is judgmental or categorical. In fact, one of the major attacks against the study of literature has been on the social implications of assessing the quality of literature. According to the spokesmen of this attack, literary criticism developed out of a social purpose—the education of the bourgeoisie who strove to gain cultural knowledge not by their own reading and thinking but by the aid of knowledgable cultural middlemen, who were willing to provide ready-made opinions. The usual date given for the advent of this kind of criticism is the early or mid-1800s. According to this interpretation, literary criticism became a business in itself, sustained by the literary magazines for the bourgeois who had come into affluence and who needed literary information and opinions in order to appear "cultured." One can find the kind of literary criticism that provides readers with ready-made opinions still, primarily in the literary magazines and reviews. Moreover, the demand that the magazine sell seems to dictate a negative approach to the work in question, and only seldom does one find a review that speaks in favor of the work.

But the student of literature must realize that judgmental reviewing which is often severe in narrow ways is only one aspect of literary criticism. Literary criticism in the wider sense of being the commentary of men who love literature goes back further than the nineteenth century; in fact, further than Anglo-European culture. To cite just two examples, there are Aristotle's work on drama and poetry and Longinus's work on poetry. Aristotle did decide that Sophocles' *Oedipus Rex* was the best Greek tragedy, but he was more interested in why it was so, and in the human importance of the drama. He said it was important because it presented the "real actions of men," that is, those universal actions common to all people and vital to the significance of their lives. He said that drama could have a therapeutic effect on the audience by calling up the emotions of pity and fear and then purging the audience of them. Longinus said that the audience could be transported by the writer's capacity to embody his own great soul in his work. Neither of these men were concerned with providing ready-made judgments for others to mouth or to think that a literary experience was a comfortable, drawing-room entertainment.

To give a more personal example, the man who taught me literary criticism was most concerned with the explication of the text. The literary work in and for itself was his most important concern, and the criterion for the quality of the work was its unity. He did not mention the life of the artist, the effect on the audience, or even the possible "truth" the work might have had or still has. And at that time, nothing could have been more important to me than his approach. For him to analyze a poem and demonstrate the amazing connections between words, sound, stanza structure, and idea was to show me how rich literature was and what artistry there was in its creation.

With any such technique as this, the value depends upon the man using it, and in the hands of mediocre critics, it can degenerate into something that students have, with justification, called "dissection." The poem becomes a mechanism which can be sorted, classified, and identified. The sensitive student who knows that a literary work is more than a mechanical toy must resist a mechanistic approach, but he must be careful that he does not also reject the rich critical possibilities which are contained in determining the interrelationships of all parts of the work as it appears on the page. It is especially important when a reader objects to "dissection" or to "tearing poems apart" that he realize that nothing is happening to his view of the work; the work will always be there, whole, inviolable, and free of stigma. He must always take what he can from other interpretations to make his own more significant, and

remember that rereading the work and experiencing its
wholeness becomes the evidence that reductive criticism de-
stroys only itself.

If a student wants to know how a literary work achieves its
effect, its relation to the experience of other readers, its place
in the history of art or society, its relation to its author, its
relation to him; or if the student is curious how people create
patterns of words so that they continue to affect other persons
ages after they have been set down and why others continue
to see value and importance in these patterns, then criticism
can be of value to him because it is the process which will lead
him toward the knowledge he desires. The literary critic,
R. P. Blackmur, once said that criticism was the work of an
amateur. He meant for his readers to remember that the root
of the word is the Latin for "to love." That is, the work of a
critic is with something he loves, perhaps as an object itself,
perhaps as the creation of one of his fellow humans. He also
meant that a good reader cannot afford to become narrow-
viewed and single-purposed, which is often the result of be-
coming the professional reader-critic. Blackmur offers a fine
analogy: "Like walking, criticism is a pretty nearly universal
art; both require a constant intricate shifting and catching of
balance; neither can be questioned much in process; and few
perform either really well." [3] Blackmur's emphasis is on flex-
ibility, on allowing the work to create its own terrain, and on
trying to match one's own perception to the path one walks.
Criticism is a tentative act that must always be suspicious of its
own capacities. Some critics and some readers of criticism
have forgotten this. But we need to remember that just as
there was, is, and always will be reductive and dogmatic criticism, so there was, is, and always will be illuminating criticism.
It is true that literary criticism has become an immense field
and that there are many more works of criticism being written now than ever before, but this does not mean that good
criticism is no longer written and that all amateurs have be-

come dogmatists. The value of criticism is not that it lays down laws which any reader must follow, but rather that it offers a new way of seeing a literary work which may not have been possible to the reader. And if it enriches his perception of a literary work, then it has value.

CHAPTER TWO

Ways of Seeing

I could not have written this chapter or this book had it not been for the demonstration of the breadth of critical inquiry that M. H. Abrams offers in *The Mirror and the Lamp*. His first chapter identifies four basic approaches to literary criticism; the mimetic, the pragmatic, the expressive, and the objective.[1] These correspond to the areas of experience that literary works are related to. The mimetic approach describes the relationship of the literary work to the world or the "universe" in which the work was conceived or is being read. The pragmatic concerns itself with the effect of the work on its audience. The expressive proposes the study of the relationship of the work to the writer. The objective approach is that which studies the work in and for itself without reference to the world in which it exists, its effect on its readers, or its relationship to the author. These four approaches are equally valid; each has its limitations, and each has value and can provide some knowledge that the others cannot. The relationship of a literary work to each of these areas of experience is permanent; therefore, the intrinsic value of each approach as an area of concern and interest cannot be denied, even though one approach may be more in fashion during a particular period.

Within any one reader's experience, the areas form their relations according to the idiosyncrasies of that reader. For example, the first response of some students of literature is to be curious about the writer. The first question for them is "Why did he write this?" Such a response sends the student to biographical and psychological studies. Then he may want to inquire into the history and culture of the period during which the author lived. As he studies those subjects, he will be led back to the work to find out further what is there and will perhaps then have recourse to an objective approach, and also ask if the work is in some way "true" to the period in which the writer lived or "true" to the artist's conception of that time. The relationship that any reader and any work can develop cannot be determined by formula; it springs out of each new meeting and the possibilities are infinite.

M. H. Abrams sets out the four approaches in order of their historical appearances, but I want to vary that order and discuss what he calls the "objective" possibilities first for two reasons: one, my own literary education really began with that approach. Two, most of the introductory anthologies and courses still stress that approach. I share their idea of the importance of the firsthand meeting with the work in itself and want to begin looking at the work from this point of view.

a.   The Work for Itself

The differences between the four ranges of critical approaches are the kinds of information and knowledge they can give the reader, not the quality of information. Critical approaches have gained and lost popularity and perhaps the only judgment that can be made of them is that some have been more important to students of literature at one period than they have been to students in another. Moreover, the preferences are usually determined by nonliterary factors, such as politics, social conditions, and philosophical or religious movements. But a good critic is not bound by the literary fashions of his time; his only limits are his own intelligence and sensitivity and that which the works he reads can engender in him. He is not even wholly bound by living in a particular period, for his range is not solely determined by the material events of his contemporary history. His study is of something outside his immediate realm (especially if he is studying literature from another period or culture). He is freed by the literature he is studying, often by the work itself, and it is the work itself that this section is about.

Abrams calls this the "objective" approach. Although the word "objective" now has connotations of a value judgment (for instance, we say that some facts or statements are more objective than others), that is not what he means by the word. "Objective" criticism means a study of the literary work done without reference to the mimetic, pragmatic, or expressive possibilities of interpretation. The objective approach regards the literary work as an object, having an independent existence and capable of allowing and supporting inquiry without reference to its origin, its mimetic capacity, or its affective possibilities. The work is important in and for itself not only because it is art, but also because it is the *work* of an artist that separates him from other persons.

I have chosen to retitle this approach because I would like to move away from both the idea of objectivity and from the connotation of the word "object." There is no way to get entirely away from subjectivity in literary study, nor would I want to. However, I do think of the initial contact as that between the reader and the work *on the page*, and also as being the source for the other inquiries. I would like to emphasize the spatial independence of the work and the idea that the possibilities of the work by itself begin *before* the other approaches enter. The phrase, the work for itself, also emphasizes the work as craft, and it is in this area that we can talk about a literary work as that carefully constructed pattern of words which is the basis for all our speculations for its truth, its revelation, and its power.

There are many ways of being concerned with the work for itself. Often this approach concerns itself with the records of the creation of a work and chooses as its focal point a study of the revisions that appear in the manuscript versions of the work. Such a study shows us the writer at work as he changes and revises, backs up and then goes on, looking for that rightness of expression that he desires. Such a study is fascinating because some changes seem to be logical ones that we can see a rationale for; other changes seem almost whimsical, but in the end absolutely correct. Take for instance the three versions of Blake's "The Tyger," which are reproduced below:

[*First Draft*]²

The Tyger

1   Tyger Tyger burning bright
         In the forests of the night
         What immortal hand or eye
         ~~Dare~~ **Could** frame thy fearful symmetry

                 Burnt in
2   ~~In what~~ distant deeps or skies
     ~~The cruel~~ **Burnt the** fire of thine eyes
         On what wings dare he aspire
         What the hand dare sieze the fire

3   And what shoulder & what art
         Could twist the sinews of thy heart
         And when thy heart began to beat
         What dread hand & what dread feet

         ~~Could fetch it from the furnace deep~~
         ~~And in thy horrid ribs dare steep~~
         ~~In the well of sanguine woe~~
         ~~In what clay & in what mould~~
         ~~Were thy eyes of fury rolld~~

4   ^{Where}
          ~~What~~ the hammer ~~what~~ ^{where} the chain
          In what furnace was thy brain

                                     ^{dread grasp}
          What the anvil what ~~the arm arm grasp clasp~~
     Dare ~~Could~~ its deadly terrors ~~clasp grasp~~ clasp

6   Tyger Tyger burning bright
          In the forests of the night
          What immortal hand & eye

             ^{frame}
          Dare ~~form~~ thy fearful symmetry

[Second Full Draft]

Tyger Tyger burning bright
In the forests of the night
What Immortal hand & eye
Dare frame thy fearful symmetry

And what shoulder & what art
Could twist the sinews of thy heart
And when thy heart began to beat
What dread hand & what dread feet

When the stars threw down their spears
And waterd heaven with their tears
Did he smile his work to see
Did he who made the lamb make thee

Tyger Tyger burning bright
In the forests of the night
What immortal hand & eye
Dare frame thy fearful symmetry

[Final Version, 1794]

Tyger! Tyger! burning bright
In the forests of the night,
What immortal hand or eye
Could frame thy fearful symmetry?

In what distant deeps or skies
Burnt the fire of thine eyes?
On what wings dare he aspire?
What the hand dare sieze the fire?

And what shoulder, & what art,
Could twist the sinews of thy heart?
And when thy heart began to beat,
What dread hand? & what dread feet?

What the hammer? what the chain?
In what furnace was thy brain?
What the anvil? what dread grasp
Dare its deadly terrors clasp?

When the stars threw down their spears,
And water'd heaven with their tears,
Did he smile his work to see?
Did he who made the Lamb make thee?

Tyger! Tyger! burning bright
In the forests of the night,
What immortal hand or eye,
Dare frame thy fearful symmetry?

By the second version, Blake had rearranged the stanzas so
that the last is an echo of the first, and the poem comes to have
a nearly ritualistic form. But what caused Blake in the last
version to change the first "Dare" to "Could" and retain the
last "Dare"? Why did he decide to put the stanza about the
hammer and the anvil back in the poem? These are questions
which we might answer by arriving at an interpretation of
the last version which would show the rightness of each
choice in order to form the work as we now know it; but that
hindsight of ours is not what led Blake to make those changes.
The record of the process is clear in the revision, but the process itself is still mysterious.

There is another kind of textual criticism which deals not
with manuscripts but with the problems of the printed text
which may arise when the manuscripts are lost and the writer
no longer alive or willing to talk. This criticism attempts to
establish the most reliable edition, that is, the one that most
nearly represents what is thought to be the author's intention.

Shakespeare's plays present the most famous examples of the importance of textual criticism. We have no copies of the playwright's original manuscripts and the editions of his plays are based on copies used by prompters or attempted reconstructions of the plays by actors or others connected with the production of the plays. How do we know what Shakespeare really wrote in some cases? The job of the textual critic is to study the texts available and to account for the irregularities and discrepancies in the hope of arriving at a version that seems closest to what the author originally intended. Without such studies, readers would often be left with inaccurate if not incoherent texts.

Both of the above critical activities are what I call descriptive ones. That is, they seek primarily to describe a text. Though editors of manuscripts and editions have to make judgments not only about interpretations but also sometimes about the quality of one reading over another, both aim not at evaluating the work itself so much as at simply presenting it. In fact, the descriptive activity is the approach to the work for itself in its simplest form. It can be employed not only on the revisions and editions of the work, but also on the finished or reliable version.

Many students know this approach to the text through an education in poetics, or prosody, that consisted of learning the basic metrical patterns and verbal effects (iambic tetrameter, couplets, alliteration, rhyme, etc.). Like any concern, the study of prosody can become an end in itself and convey only a mechanical, statistical response to literature. But it need not be so. The study of prosody, which is part of the study of poetic style, and the study of prose style, serves to remind us of a vital aspect of the writer's art. He is not simply one who writes down thoughts or ideas; he is a craftsman of sound and effect as well as of ideas. There is a definition of poetry that might be extended to fiction if not to expository prose as well: "The right words in the right order." Writers are concerned with the patterns of their ideas as well as with the ideas themselves. Poets are concerned not only with word order but with sound and the effects of sound, and when we concern ourselves with those devices, then we concern ourselves with what writers are interested in also.

Another approach to the work for itself is that of generic criticism. Instead of being interested only with the use of various devices of metrics and sound, we can also be interested in the *types* of literature. The broadest categories are ones such as plays, novels, poems. However, most genre studies are those of genres within the larger ones just mentioned. The largest number of generic approaches are those to poems, because there are more genres and they are more clearly established by traditions of use. There are the conventions of the elegy, sonnet, epic, ode, sestina, and others, as well as genres of individual parts of poems, such as stanzas, particular kinds of similes, line lengths, and the like. The concern of generic studies is often both historical and individual. What happens to a specific genre or convention of form as it is passed on from one writer to the next can often tell us something not only of the individual poet's response to convention but also of his and his age's response to the concepts of convention, tradition, and inherited forms. We know something important about a writer when we know whether he considers himself a part of a tradition or whether he considers himself to be starting anew with no obligation to the writers that have come before or to the convention of the particular kind of writing that he is doing. But the value of the concern with genres may also be in demonstrating the uniqueness of individual works. In such cases there is no value in using a word to define a work (elegy, tragedy, novel) merely to assign it to a category. That is reductive criticism. But insofar as such terms are used as norms by which to perceive the poet's own inventiveness and his new use of such forms to mold a work that is his own, then they are of use.

There are also descriptive approaches which concern themselves not with the elements which make up a work, but with the resulting product. One such possibility is the determination of the theme or central idea of a work. A thematic approach attempts to bring the various aspects of *form* as well as content together to make a statement about the subject of a work and it may also concern itself with the message or moral of that work. A concern for the work itself need not be only with the poetic devices. Part of a literary work is its meaning and an approach to the work for itself must of course be willing to involve that too. Such a concern becomes mimetic when it attempts to generalize by placing the meaning of the work in some kind of historical or cultural context, though it may be argued that any concern with meaning is also a concern for importance or significance and thus is automatically mimetic. What matters here is that we understand how such an approach can root itself in a study of the text and gradually evolve into a wider study.

A more specific kind of objective approach is one which not only describes the work but which seeks as a result of that description to assess its consistency or unity. The concept of unity in a literary work is not always clearly formulated by those who wish to find it; in fact, there may be several kinds of unity. There is unity of theme—that is, all the work is about the same topic. There is unity of imagery—all the images contribute to the same general vision or implication, theme, or "central image." There is unity of tone. There is unity of form. This last is a vague notion, but generally it means that the parts of the work can be said to fit together and mutually support each other.

The unity of form became a special focus for a particular school of criticism, the New Criticism, that traces its theory back to Coleridge, who formulated and described the concept of "organic unity," employing the image of the plant to describe both poet and poem. However, Coleridge's concept of form actually begins from an expressive concern, for he says that the power of unity is to be found in the poet, where it

. . . reveals itself in the balance or reconciliation of opposite or discordant qualities: of sameness, with difference; of the general, with the concrete; the idea, with the image; the individual, with the representative; the sense of novelty and freshness, with the old and familiar objects . . . and while it blends and harmonizes the natural and artificial, still subordinates art to nature; the manner to the matter; and our admiration of the poet to our sympathy with the poetry.

Here we may see the power of Coleridge's expressive point of view. His study and his analogies come from his sense of the vital relationship of the poet to the poem, and he transfers his sense of the capacities of the poet to a concept of the form of the poem:

But if the definition sought for be that of *legitimate* poem, I answer, it must be one, the parts of which mutually support and explain each other; all in their proportion harmonizing with, and supporting the purpose and known influences of metrical arrangement . . .[3]

The New Criticism translated Coleridge's statement from one about the process to one solely about the product, and said, in its strictest interpretations, that all parts of a literary work must have internal connections. There can be no loose ends, no excrescence. The discovery of the unity of the poem became the goal of the analytical process, and the judgment of the quality of the work was based on its degree of unity.

The New Criticism seems to have come into being partly as a result of certain modern philosophical assumptions. The least worthy of the reasons for its popularity may have been a desire on the part of its practitioners to find a critical method capable of the same kind of verifiability as the scientific method possesses. But the objective approach may be traced back to some of the same esthetic origins as modern literature itself. It has been said that with the disappearance of a community of religious belief in the mid- and late-1700s, the artist saw that his task was not to create a microcosm which was analogous and thus derivative of the world which was the macrocosm made by God. He now saw his task as that of creating a world which would be its own macrocosm, and the artist himself became the creator. Each work is in itself a universe which is complete within itself and which generates its own coherence. Consequently, if a literary work can generate its own meaning by virtue of its internal coherence, then a critical method can concern itself with that esthetic universe. This is beginning to sound vaguely "existentialist;" however, we are talking not about the welter of daily experience, but about literary and artistic forms. If we assume, as Blackmur says, that "Art is life at the remove of form and meaning," then the creation of a work of art, bringing some kind of coherence or order out of experience, is what we may call "existentialist." However, the creative process does not need philosophical credentials, nor can any system fully account for it. In fact, the concern for art as an object and the interest in that aspect is as old as art itself.

The long popularity of the New Criticism has had its bad effects, the worst being that in the hands of some critics it became a kind of weighing and balancing act often accompanied by an unspoken assumption that once analysis was done, there was nothing more to be said about a literary work. Hence, many readers came to feel that literary criticism consisted of "tearing works apart" or "dissection." At the very least, literary works became mechanical toys for the delight of those whose interest was in cogs, wheels, and levers.

It is right to disavow reductive criticism that does not allow the full range of the literary work to affect the full range of the reader's capacities, but the New Criticism is no more wholly bad than any other critical approach. In the hands of sensitive critics, the tools of the New Criticism, careful reading and concentrated thought about the work itself, taught students of literature two extraordinarily valuable things. First of all, its method consisted of an explication of the text to determine the interconnections of all parts of the work, not leaving them separated into form and content or other small parcels. That method taught us how to read closely and carefully. It gave us a way of concentrating on the text. For me, the method offered a revelation of how rich in possibilities a work could be and how rewarding literary study could be. I still have great pleasure in discovering for myself the internal connections of a poem. Its second great value was that its emphasis on the work returned readers' attention to the art of literature itself—away from the many exterior approaches, which though valuable, are so only because there is a literary work at the center of them. The work should stand at the center of the reader's study. All the knowledge that the reader accumulates about its history, its author, its appeal or effect, has the work itself for its living center. Consequently, for the reader whose knowledge has grown out from that center, the work evokes not only the feelings and associations that it contains in itself, but also the emotion and knowledge of all the insight and information that the reader has acquired as a result of the study of that work and its related areas. There is no other experience like that one, and it can always be recalled because the work has the stability of form, but the power of always growing in significance.

There is another possibility that I would like to set out: A friend who writes fiction once told me that he believed there was a kind of criticism that sees the work not from the reader's point of view but from the writer's. His simplest example was that when the reader talks about "plot," the writer talks about the "movement" or "sequence" of a work. It is a critical possibility of great value and manifests itself most often in writing workshops rather than in courses comprised of reading literature. Here is Auden speaking of apprentice writers reading each other's works:

The apprentices do each other a further mutual service which no older and sounder critic could do. They read each other's manuscripts. At this age a fellow apprentice has two great virtues as a critic. When he reads your poem, he may grossly overestimate it, but if he does, he really believes what he is saying; he never flatters or praises merely to encourage. Secondly, he reads your poem with that passionate attention which grown-up critics only give to masterpieces and grown-up poets only to themselves. When he finds fault, his criticisms are intended to help you improve. He really wants your poem to be better.[4]

What more can one desire of a critic than that he wishes the work to be at its best, and why reserve that quality of mind only for apprentices? It's not a question of what the meaning of the work is. It's not an examination of the intellectual structure of the work or its prosody in order to find out what the poem or the poet believes. It is the human act of desiring that what a man has made be as good as it can possibly be. Auden speaks of "passionate attention." That is required of any critic from any critical stance.

Those who have heard a group of writers reading to each other and reading each other's work and commenting on it, realize that it can be as reductive as any kind of criticism. In fact, it can be the most destructive because it can strike down a promising work in progress or destroy a friendship that might have been the catalyst for excellent work. On the other hand, it is also capable of being one of the most beautifully delicate of activities, for it involves not only the integrity of the work and the intelligence and sensitivity of the reader, but also the personalities of both writer and reader. When it is well done it has about it the magnanimity and charity that all human relationships should possess. To the student who does not write the kind of literature he studies, I offer the writer's approach to criticism as one of the most enlightening. The requisite is that the student begin writing some of his own verse, fiction, or what have you, to get a sense of the sheer labor involved. The result is that questions of form and meaning will have the composition of the work as their context, and the demands and the possibilities of the writing process will offer further insight into the work as it is offered to the reader.

I have great regard for the critical approach that is primarily concerned with the work for itself. Unless the core of the study of a literary work is the work itself, it is not literary study. It may be historical, biographical, philosophical, or whatever, and all those have value. But those other studies are important to the work only if the work is the central object. Nevertheless, the other possibilities are not made less by the initial emphasis on the work for itself, and they provide insight and comprehensiveness of view that makes the study of the work for itself a more rewarding one.

b.   The Mimetic Possibilities

The word "mimetic" is derived from *mimesis*, which means imitation. However, it has come to mean something more specific when applied to literary inquiry. Mimetic criticism is that which asks how a literary work is important to any of the worlds to which it is related, and the best place to begin a survey of the possible mimetic approaches is with the connections between the work and the time in which it was written.

A study of the relationship of a literary work to its contemporary cultures is one of the most demanding. If we pursue this inquiry, our task is to discover the extent to which the content or form of a work departs or conforms to the values, ideas, or literary conventions of its day. Any assessment involves steeping oneself in the history, philosophy, esthetics, or in other words, in the cultural world of the work. Only after that can one begin to answer the questions about the relationship of the work to the period. There are ways in which this approach offers knowledge of inestimable value, for it takes the reader out of his own culture into another one and demands that he become a person who can at least partially assimilate the values of the age in which the work was written.

But the approach also has hidden difficulties. Often the idea of the history and culture of the period has been formulated through a study of those same literary works which the reader wishes to assess. Sometimes the histories of a period use literary works as their basis for interpretation; therefore, instead of discovering the relation of the period to the work, the reader of those histories only revolves in a great circle of scholarship. The way out of this circle is through the study of other contemporary documents. For instance, one way of discovering the extent to which the plays of Shakespeare are consistent with the cultural life of Renaissance England would be to study contemporary historical records such as court documents or diaries; another would be to study plays by Christopher Marlowe and Ben Jonson in order to discover the common elements of the plays, or to study late medieval plays in order to determine Shakespeare's use of dramatic devices from earlier plays, or the extent to which the content of his plays was similar to and perhaps derived from medieval ideas. Students with more modern preferences would be well rewarded by studying nineteenth-century novels against a background of reading in Marx and Freud. The purpose of such a study would not be to prove that any novelist was a Marxist or a Freudian, but it might very well show the extent to which the economic and psychological thought embodied in the works of Marx and Freud was part of the intellectual currency of the age, and thus go far to exemplify the uniqueness of the particular novels.

One problem of determining a work's relation to its own period is that of deciding if the final outcome of the study is to be a statement about the relationship between the artist and the audience, or the work and the audience. To take them in order: A study of the period may yield information about the relationship of the artist and his audience, but it is important to distinguish not only between the public's sentiments and the artist's, but also between the various possible audiences which the artist may have had. We can not always define precisely the audience on whom our notions of the time should be based. Should we assume that Shakespeare's audience were those people who crowded into the Globe Theater (as though they were all of the same class or cultural level!) or the members of the royal court who watched some of his private productions? On the other hand, a study of the cultural milieu may bypass the author himself and attempt to establish a relationship between the ideas in the work and the ideas of the culture. But that approach is subject to the same limitations as the study of the artist and the audience, for it assumes that there is a single audience during a particular time that can be defined, studied, and affirmed as the one to which the ideas in the work must be compared.

These critical possibilities have their values as well as their limitations. Their danger is in the assumption that a literary work has a direct correlation with the society in which it was written, which is to say that it is not the product of an individual, but more like a document generated out of a committee meeting. But these approaches are valuable when the relations are defined carefully, for they demonstrate that the possibilities of the relationships between the artist, his work, and his own culture are infinite.

The purpose of such studies as those outlined above does not include an attempt to define the applicability or significance of past literary works to the present time. Historical studies of literature will not in themselves tell us how the works in question pertain to an audience of a later period. Yet the study of a work's significance to our own time is a popular one now and we need to learn what assumptions such studies make and what the potential of those studies is.

There are two ways in which literature of the past may have value to the present. First, the relation may be based on co-incidence. Certain political, historical, or cultural events of the past may appear similar to those of our own time and thus it may be of value to discover what men who were subject to those previous events thought about them. Two examples of works about coincidental subjects come to mind, Dickens's *Hard Times* and Wilfred Owen's "Dulce et Decorum Est." Dickens's novel is about the social and spiritual evils that attended the rise of industrial capitalism in England. We can find in the work attacks on the kind of mechanical "facts and figures" education that many writers of our own time are attacking and we can also find there an examination of the relations between labor and management. Owen's poem does not present quite the same problems. The poem is a narrative by a man who has seen others die in gas attacks during war. The point of the poem is that once you have seen what the narrator has, the terrible death agonies caused by chlorine gas, you will not believe "the old lie" that "it is sweet and proper to die for one's country." The poem has tremendous shock value and its message has much power among those who feel that war is a personal crime and tragedy and not an affair of national honor. We may take both novel and poem as examples of works that speak to situations similar to those that many of us find ourselves in now.

The events may look similar to those that a modern audience encounters but they are actually of different times and different cultures. Therefore, if we wish to use Dickens's insight into the problems of industrialization in early nineteenth-century England in order to aid our insight into our problems, then our questions must be directed toward searching out exactly what it is Dickens is attacking and what he offers as solutions or alternatives. We must also ask ourselves if his solutions are possible solutions either for the situation that he describes or for our own. Are the situations really the same? Are the plights of those who suffer so similar that we can over-look the difference in time (about a hundred years) and place (England rather than the United States)? Owen's poem, on the other hand, does not arouse the same skepticism about its relationship to our own time even though it is about a past war (World War I) and about a chlorine gas attack. First of all, there seems little possibility of questioning the similarity of all modern wars, and today we are still much involved in discussions about chemical warfare. But the themes seem even more basic—the death of a man through warfare and its effect on another individual. These seem to be universal experiences, and when a reader affirms their universality, then he is assert-ing the second kind of relationship that may pertain between past and present. That is, there are elements of human life that do not change and that not only does the literary work embody those qualities, but they are preserved in the reader's own time. Such an affirmation demands a moral, philosophic, or psychological commitment. The value of literature, in fact the value of language itself, is based on the faith in a common human experience which can be communicated or evoked through literature. For if language does not furnish common experience through its relationship to some enduring part of human nature, then we are only gibbering idiots who have no capacity for dealing with the world except through action, while we are in fact alone.

One of the oldest assertions in western literature affirming the possibility of mimetic inquiry through universal values is Aristotle's statement that the form of a tragic drama is "an imitation of the real actions of men." Without a psychological or historical-anthropological theory behind him, Aristotle af-firmed simply that the actions of men have a permanence about them that allows a tragedy to be applicable to men in general and that a play, composed of action and language, has the capacity to convey that applicability. His is a moral statement; it is concerned with how men behave and implies that the possible actions of men are finite and therefore repeated from one age to the next.

The basis for Aristotle's statement about the mimetic truth of tragedy is cultural and religious. The play on which he based his idea of tragedy was Sophocles' *Oedipus Rex*. We know that play and others were originally presented during the springtime rites of fertility and regeneration. One idea about the permanent mimetic significance of the play is that it reiterates the age-old rite of the sacrifice of a scapegoat, a sacrifice which cleansed the city and allowed the women to bear children and the crops to grow anew. Given this explanation of the cultural origins of the play, the basic pattern of its action is natural, religious, and is mimetically "true" because it is based on permanent patterns of human social behavior. It is natural because it links peoples' lives with the cycle of seasons and with the necessity for the end of winter and the coming of spring. It is religious because it became a part of the religious rites which involved the all-important function of supplication for the health of the community. It is cultural because it manifests an element of society that still exists. For instance, in order to demonstrate the continuing validity of the play, some interpreters suggest that the basic pattern of the scapegoat ritual may still be found in the pattern of events surrounding Christ's trial, death, and resurrection. This kind of study and interpretation that attempts to tie literary works to basic patterns in cultures or peoples' minds is called archetypal criticism. Its mimetic possibilities lie in the connections that can be demonstrated between the literary work and cultural or behavioral patterns that can be discovered throughout a historical period or a culture.

It is only a short distance from the archetypal criticism which is based on the evidence of archaeological and anthropological studies to archetypal criticism based on myth, for myth has its roots in peoples' cultural and religious responses to events in their lives. In fact, the distinction I draw here is not one that archetypal critics usually draw. However, we may for the time being see that another possible approach to literature through permanent cultural patterns may involve a study of the archetypes preserved in mythology. An example of the common ground which "anthropological" criticism and mythic criticism share is *Oedipus Rex*, for the story of Oedipus became a myth, and other works which follow the basic pattern of this myth are said to contain the "oedipal" pattern. There the archetypal pattern is said to be the unconscious conflict of the father and son for the mother's love, a psychological archetype. Another example of the psychological archetype that becomes myth is the basic pattern of a son's search for his father, which is embodied in the story of Telemachus, Odysseus' son. The pattern of the man who challenges the gods for the sake of other men is known as the Promethean myth. Another pattern is that of the quest, and critics and historians have spent much time demonstrating the permanence of this archetypal pattern in mythology and literature. The continuing attractiveness of archetypal criticism can be seen in existentialist critics' revival of the myth of Sisyphus. Because he disobeyed the gods, Sisyphus was punished by being forced to roll a huge boulder up the slope of a mountain. When he had almost reached the top, the boulder would roll down again, and he was forced to repeat this eternally. The fate of this character is said to be the fate of all living people. Consequently, the pattern of Sisyphus' punishment is often seen as underlying the fate of contemporary fictional heroes who persevere in the face of certain failure.

Yet another kind of mimetic criticism is based not on theories of human nature or values, or on permanent patterns of behavior, but on theories of history. In fact, though the study of history can be separated from the study of literature and vice versa, very few theories of literature or criticism exist outside a notion of what the history of mankind means or what the direction of history is. The image of history varies with each individual, but there are a few basic patterns. History may be merely a narrative of events. That is, the point of view may be indicated by transitions of a merely chronological nature, an "and then" sequence. The implication of this structure is that the events of human history have no inherent meaning, but are simply random events in time and space. Such a view makes it necessary for each individual to interpret events for himself. But more likely, the transition in any historical view will be "because" or "as a result of" or "eventually." Here, the assumption is that there is a cause-effect sequence in history. Out of this usually comes either a "downward" or an "upward" sense of history.

When applied to literature, the theory of decline usually results in an emphasis upon the imitation of past cultures or literary works. The imitator assumes that if the past is superior to the present, then it is best to imitate or preserve what has gone before. Moreover, such imitation may help stave off further decline. For the critic, this often means comparing his own contemporary literature with that of the past and judging whether that of the present meets the standards of the past. In contrast, those who believe in the theory of improvement usually assume that the past was inferior to the present and that culture and civilization have constantly improved and ennobled people. When applied to literature, this theory emphasizes originality and newness. There is often a rejection of the past as being simply irrelevant; any imitation of past literature is nothing less than an attempt to impede development.

There are also some variations of the upward and downward theories that deserve mention. The upward theory of history became for some the belief in "progress," and though this notion gained its real power in the nineteenth century, it is no less powerful today. Literature, for those who believe in progress, is evaluated in terms of its contribution to material improvement. Purely imaginative literature is regarded as a waste of time; it does not tell men how to build, buy, or how to "grow more potatoes." Literature which affirms individual variation, idiosyncrasies, or the right of the individual to remain outside society is considered "subversive," for progress depends upon the smooth workings of society. Literature exposing unpleasant social or economic conditions is bad if it does so at the expense of progress. If it allows progress to continue or even to proceed at a greater rate, it is good.

But the belief in progress also generated another way of looking at literature. Marxist critics, for example, do not reject the notion of literature reflecting progress, but they redefine progress, so that it will aid the worker rather than the manufacturer. Thus, the subject of literature was to be changed from "progress" to the "class struggle;" and in later Marxist theories, the content of literature was required to anticipate the eventual victory of the working classes. Here then was a mimetic approach founded on the historical and sociological assumption that the end of history can be foreseen and that the end will be a fulfillment of human hopes.

One of the effects of a theory of literature based upon a foreseeable direction or end to history is the argument from posterity. Persons who use this argument justify their judgments or actions by appealing to what is to come. The end justifies the means, and since the end is evident only to a chosen few, there is no need to explain one's position or for an opponent to understand. History will exonerate any judgment made or action done in the name of the future. In criticism, such a judgment is often voiced as: "This work will still be read by generations to come" or "This won't last."

I began this book by saying that the study of literature cannot take place outside the context of human values. There is perhaps no more abiding assumption of human values than a person's concept of history itself, for that involves an estimate not only of oneself but also of the whole community of mankind, not only in this time, but in all time, whatever one considers that time to include. It must be emphasized that a belief in the direction of history is no more or less than that, a belief. A direction cannot be proven other than to trace one in the past, but even that pattern of past events is not evidence for a pattern in the future. In a literary context, the student cannot defend or refute the value of a work according to what it will be. He can and must see it only in terms of what it is at his own point in time.

One other kind of mimetic criticism deserves to be mentioned here, though it is not a separate type. I have heard many students demand that what they read have personal significance for them—the word is usually "relevance." It seems to me that part of this demand has come about because literary study has frequently become a process of pigeonholing literary works in such a way as to neglect affirming a basic reason for reading literature—that it can become important to people because they wish to and can see their own lives in it. However, the resulting demand for relevance is often also carried too far by insisting that the only literature of value is about local issues. It is always pertinent to ask if some literary work from the past or from a different cultural or racial world has any significance to an individual not of that time or those places. But it is also necessary for that same reader to ask if that literary work should not become important to him whether he is immediately engaged in its ideas or not.

There is yet one more possibility for mimetic criticism and in some ways the most difficult of all because it requires not a mere commitment but a leap of faith. That possibility is that humans continue to affirm the same moral values in age after age. Thus, the student must be willing to say not only that people have remained basically the same in their cultural, psychological, and physical make-up, but that their morality has also remained stable. As a result, the literature that a student reads from any period in the past will affirm his own morality. The latest large critical inquiry in this area has been the existentialist approach to literature, which has moved from present to past in order to demonstrate that not only Sartre and Camus, but also Robert Browning, and even Shakespeare and Chaucer have embodied existential concepts in their work. One problem with this kind of criticism is that it often sacrifices the literary work to a philosophical doctrine, a not uncommon tendency in any critical theory. Often existentialist critics neglect a fundamental aspect of all art when they attempt to find what they call the "existential" aspect of the work. The notion that the artist brings order out of chaos or through his effort brings something into being that has meaning *only* after it is created, which is somewhat analogous to Sartre's "existence before essence," is fundamental to esthetic creation, but it in no way affirms the artist's philosophical commitment to existentialism. It merely means that he is an *artist*, involved not just in sustaining life, but in creating it.

Readers who do not find existentialism particularly inviting as a means of examining the meaning of a work may wish to resort to more basic and seemingly more lasting systems of values, such as Christian morality. Or they may wish to derive a statement that seems to affirm the basic morality of western culture and to study the relations of what they are reading to that formulation. But whatever assumptions the reader makes about the relationship of literature to mankind at large, they remain only assumptions. Those who think that criticism is a science or that it can be certain of its assumptions or dogma forget the essential relation of literature to people—it is founded on human values whose certainty lies only in the faith that language can somehow allow individuals to share their private experiences. Any critic must realize that criticism is not the exemplification of a law but an affirmation of belief. Criticism at its best is an act of courage.

c. The Affective Possibilities

The word Abrams uses to describe this approach is "pragmatic." I have changed the heading to "affective," a word he also uses, because that word seems to me to encompass more of the possibilities for the effect of a work on the reader. The word "pragmatic" has come to mean "useful" in too narrow a sense, even though Abrams does not use it that way. He remarks that a "pragmatic theory . . . looks at the work of art chiefly as a means to an end, an instrument for getting something done, and tends to judge its value according to its success in achieving that aim." But his statement does not mean that literary works are how-to manuals or propaganda. He indicates that the affective possibilities include all the ways (emotionally, intellectually, unconsciously, etc.) that literature may affect one. Thus, this approach concerns itself with that which has been said to separate *literature* from other kinds of writing and *art* from what is only competence or technique or important subject matter. In the most general sense, the affective concern is the concern for what in art moves us, and that capacity is sometimes described in the most emotional of terms. Emily Dickinson says that she knows when what she is reading is a poem because she feels as though the top of her head is coming off. That statement may seem extreme; nevertheless it is true that art serves more than the function of disseminating information or teaching. Coleridge says that literature contributes to a feeling of bodily as well as mental convalescence. Men have tried to find a term for that feeling since they have thought about the effects of art: *beauty*, the *sublime, uplifting*, have all been tried. The feeling I have is often that of having received a gift, and it may be that gift of enriched feelings that has led to the study of literature, for

study brings about renewed contact with the source of en-
larged emotional capacity. It is the affective quality of literature that often seems most personal of all its qualities, yet it
is also the affective quality of a work that often creates the
greatest desire in the reader to share that work and the experience of reading it with someone else. The paradox is the
desire to share the most private.

However, even though this approach concerns itself with
the study that often seems most personally valuable, it is
heavily dependent upon the mimetic approach, just as the
power of literature is partially dependent on its statement. If
literature were like music, the affective possibilities could be
separated from the mimetic. But words are not like musical
notes; they have independent connotations and denotations regardless of their relationships with other words. The effect of
the combination of words is not only dependent upon their
arrangement and subsequent sound and meaning, but also
upon the individual intrinsic meanings of words. Consequently, how we are moved by literature has to do with the
extent to which the words that comprise a work possess mimetic values for us, that is, the capacity to strike us as com-
prehensible and "true."

It is the fundamental assumption of affective theories that
there is something in the work that gives it a common ground
with its audience, whether it be its contemporary audience or
ours. At times the common ground may be as superficial or
temporary as the mutual participation in a short-lived event—
for instance, a common participation in an election campaign.
From that common ground can spring a unity of interests
otherwise nonexistent, such that even the most inaccurate and
irrational propagandistic writing might be accepted as true. At
other times (I hope more often in the case of literature), the
common ground may be the appeal to fundamental aspects
of human nature such as the emotions of pity and fear which

Aristotle based his affective theory on, and which know no historical or cultural boundaries. But regardless of what the common ground is, there must be the possibility of identification. Literature must have the mimetic quality of resembling some aspect of life, though that is not to say that it must be narrowly realistic. The quality of similarity may be unconscious; it may be mythic or archetypal; it may be an event which the writer and reader have in common, either coincidentally or typically; it may even be a use of a conventional grammatical structure. But something in the work must be recognizable enough that its readers will regard the work as pertinent to their own lives before they can be affected by it. But we are now speaking of the audience and our concern is no longer with the source of a work's common ground with it, but with the affective capacity of the work, which we may see in the context of several ranges of possibilities.

There are two ways to approach the affective function of a work. One is from the point of view of what the author wants to do. The second is from the point of view of what the work does.

The initial experience of reading a literary work is a private one. In fact, some writers have the private effects chiefly in mind; their desire is to change the perceptions of their individual readers, to give them a new way of looking at an experience or even a new experience. Others see that as only the beginning, the end result being not only experience in itself, but also meaning. Perhaps the best statement of this latter is Joseph Conrad's:

My task which I am trying to achieve is, by the power of the written word to make your hear, to make you feel—it is, before all, to make you *see*. That—and no more, and it is everything. If I succeed, you shall find there according to your deserts: encouragement, consolation, fear, charm—all you demand—and perhaps, also that glimpse of **truth** for which you have forgotten to ask.[5]

Conrad moves from the point of individual perception through the affective possibilities of his work to the more general mimetic goal of truth. Yet the process he defines suggests the unity of the act of reading, the experience of the work, and the truth arrived at.

But there are other writers who desire not only to change the perceptions of individual readers, but also to change the perceptions of all their readers in such a way as to move them to collective action. To use the popular distinction, some wish to change men's minds; others wish to change the world men live in. These are not mutually exclusive intentions; in fact, it might be argued that one has to change men's minds before the world around them can be changed. But the writer's primary goal sometimes passes to that of public instruction and social reform, and when it does, he is beset with a different mimetic and pragmatic task. He must not only present a believable world to the individual reader, but that world must be similar enough to the reader's social and historical world that the necessity and possibility for action will be clear. The writer must create a public effect rather than a private one, and he must limit the range of individual private responses. A wide range of possible effects will not do for this kind of literature. The author is not concerned with his readers as individuals but as an affected and active group, which will upon having read his work, focus its energies in a particular way. Moreover, the world that the writer advocating public reform presents must be large enough or public enough to affect a sufficient number of readers to bring about that change. Most of the literature of public effect is nonfiction prose, and at present this kind of writing seems to be increasing. But occasionally a writer will use his work to comment upon and encourage change in a social or public situation. One of the best examples of this kind of literature, though now a somewhat dated one, is Upton Sinclair's *The Jungle*, an expose of the conditions in the meatpacking houses in

Chicago in the early 1900s. The public outcry that the book produced brought about the creation of the Food and Drug Administration. A contemporary example of a somewhat different affective purpose is James Michener's *The Drifters*, a novel about contemporary young people. Though the novel does not urge social reform, it does hope to create a sympathy among adults for a group of young people who seem alienated from conventional culture. Allen Ginsberg's *Howl* is a kind of expose of modern society which attempts to bring about change by making its readers aware of the cultural degeneration of American life. Likewise, there are many black poets and novelists who see their function to be the affirmation of the unique qualities of black culture. The affirmation aims to be a source of pride for black people in general and consequently an impetus for liberation. The prime example of poetry as an active, physical force in Ameer Baraka's (LeRoi Jones) insistence in his poem *Black Art* that he wants "Assassin poems, Poems that shoot / guns. Poems that wrestle cops into alleys / and take their weapons leaving them dead . . ." [6] Here Baraka has turned the affective power of literature back into the work; the poem itself not the reader is the agent for change and has become a living being. Black Art is a force *for*, not just through, its people.

There is also a kind of literature that has a strong social intent but which is not didactic in the usual sense of the word. The poet realizes that all change must begin in the individual reader, but that it can move a collective audience. I have found that note specifically in a poem by Adrienne Rich. The poem is "Planetarium," and is about Caroline Herschel, an astronomer. The last section of the poem reads:

> I have been standing all my life in the
> direct path of a battery of signals
> the most accurately transmitted most
> untranslateable language in the universe
> I am a galactic cloud so deep   so invo-

luted that a light wave could take 15
years to travel through me   And has
taken   I am an instrument in the shape
of a woman trying to translate pulsations
into images   for the relief of the body
and the reconstruction of the mind.[7]

That the poet sees herself as an "instrument" indicates that
the "relief" and "reconstruction" she desires is for all women.
Her intent is strong, and at times even broader. She writes in
"Implosions," to *all* who read it: "I wanted to choose words
that even you / would have to be changed by . . ." There
are an increasing number of contemporary poets who build
their hope for reconstruction and liberation on touching their
individual readers personally.

One aspect of the study of the effects of a work is the historical one. Generally, this involves a study of documents
contemporary with the work, such as diaries, reviews, other
literature, and historical events, in order to determine the extent of the influence that the work had either on its readers or
on other writers of the period. The study of social change
caused by literature is only one kind of historical study; there
is also the study of literary influence. There are many such
studies, not only of the influence of major figures on minor
figures, but also of the influence of minor figures on major
ones. An exciting discovery for me was the extent to which
Milton's *Paradise Lost* shaped the thinking and the works of
writers of all kinds, poets, novelists, and dramatists, from the
late 1600s well into the 1800s. Such a study makes one aware
of the great power of a literary work to shape the history of
literature and even culture at large.

Another of the affective approaches is to study the extent
to which a work is most concerned with giving pleasure or
providing instruction. If we concern ourselves with the appeal
of the work to a historically defined audience, we will discover information of primarily historical and social value be-

cause our inquiries will be in terms of: Who read this? How did they feel upon having read it? How many read this? What happened as a result of their having done so? On the other hand, if we couch our inquiries in terms of whether the work primarily gives pleasure or seeks to instruct, then we will ask questions of the work itself. Does it offer a moral, political, or social statement? This is a mimetic question, but it is necessary for the following: Does the work do so in a way as to merely elucidate the issues or is the statement couched in language that will move its audience to action? Does it use its emotional content to create belief or is the emotion an end in itself? Here again we must move out of a singularly pragmatic approach, because the affective qualities depend upon the devices as well as the message in a work. What are the affective devices of its language? What rhetorical techniques does the work employ? Is the content capable of being interpreted only by those involved in the exact historical situation the work describes, or is the content such that historical events contained can be interpreted in symbolic ways and thus appeal to readers who are removed from those immediate events? We may also be involved in a judgment of the legitimacy of the emotional appeal and in the validity of the ideas that we are being instructed in.

Yet another affective approach is to study the range of effects from the emotional to the intellectual. I do not want to imply that there is a separateness of the emotional and intellectual aspects of persons; however, there is a distinction between works which engage us primarily at the emotional levels, which attempt to recreate emotions through words, and those that engage us at more rational and detached levels. There is also the range between such extremes. Some poems do not support a skein of thought, and we are wrong in insisting that they should. Yet we cannot and should not let all poems or literary works pass for their sheer emotional power. If a work seems to concern itself with ideas, then it is our task to find out what they are and how well they are sustained within the fabric of the work. An example of a work with both emotional force and idea is John Donne's "Batter My Heart, Three Person'd God" which is a powerful emotional statement to most readers even if they do not understand the doctrinal content. But the poem is also a conscious statement of the narrator's complex relation to God through the personages of the Holy Trinity. It is legitimate in an inquiry into this poem to be concerned not only with the poetics and their affective quality but also with the theological statements. The approaches I have surveyed above are similar because they all permit a detached point of view on the part of the critic. Insofar as its concern is either historical or with the work as an object (even if it is an object capable of arousing emotion), an approach does not require that the critic's own response to a work become a part of the discussion.

But there are literary works which move us in such a way that our chief desire is to convey that excitement we derive from reading them to others. Such an approach is sometimes belittled as "appreciation," with the implication that that exercise is less important than those exercises that provide information of a historical, theoretical, or technical nature. However, I believe we should welcome the approach and give it a stronger name—"celebration." It is the quality to excite that distinguishes art from mere writing and it is that quality that I look to as being the greatest affirmation of language in the hands of an artist. That is not to say that there is no danger in the celebration of a work, for such an approach in its simplest form does not allow us to separate moral literature from immoral literature, truth from propaganda, or maudlin sentimentality from legitimate emotion. Again, it is necessary to move to a mimetic approach in order to give foundation to the affective reading. Nevertheless, if one is moved by a work of art, the affective power of the work is a prime concern; conveying that power is an important part of the critical task.

The determination of the power of a work is simple; it either affects us or it doesn't. If it doesn't, then to manufacture a response is wrong. However, it has happened many times that only after several readings, or even a period of years, have I been affected by a work that I have studied for other reasons. When I have been affected by the work and choose to make that the focus of my criticism, then I feel that I am facing one of the most difficult kinds of critical tasks, for I have a twofold integrity to maintain. I must maintain the integrity of the work by making sure that I do not distort its literal statements or even its implications insofar as I am able to determine them. I must also maintain my own integrity by not distorting my response through simplification or confusion. Nor should this attempt to convey feeling be narrowly interpreted; the feeling may be a highly intellectualized sense of the ideas embodied as well as it may be a simple almost sensory response to sound patterns. The critic must somehow find a combination of his own words and those of the work he is discussing to create meaning and convey the emotions he experiences when he reads the work; and if they involve historical or biographical knowledge, then he must find a way of incorporating that information so that it does not simply accumulate but actually contributes to the sense of wholeness of response that he wishes to create. He must not be false to the work in question, but he must nevertheless engender through his own writing an emotional climate that will lead his reader not only to an understanding but also to an appreciation of the work he is writing about. Within the framework of this approach that I have outlined, a book reviewer who likes the book he is reviewing should make his readers desire to read the book, not merely feel that by reading the review, they know the contents of the book. A scholar or critic who likes the work he is discussing should make his readers want to read the work in order that they might add his insight to their own experience and insight.

As I have pointed out in this section, the affective approaches and the mimetic approaches overlap. That is because the determination of a work's affective power depends as much upon the capacity of a work to be true to some aspect of life as it does upon devices and techniques of presentation. Moreover, it is the integral relationship of the mimetic and the affective through the nature of language that keeps the pragmatic out of the realm of pure subjectivity and allows the reader's emotional response to gain an increased richness and profundity instead of making it spiral in on itself to the point that the study of the response becomes more important than the work itself.

The pursuit of an inquiry in the one frame necessitates a pursuit of a related subject in the other. It might also be said that any approach done without the passion of an excited reader founders into dullness and pedantry. If literature itself is born in a matrix of idea and emotion and purports to affect the same matrices in its readers, then the relationship of the mimetic and the affective approaches is a wholly natural one. However, when we go to the next area of possibilities, the relationship of the work to its writer, the proportions of concern change. We will no longer be concerned with an assessment of the effects of a literary work though we will be concerned from time to time with the mimetic possibilities of it.

d.   The Expressive Possibilities

"I wanted to find out more about his poetry so I got a book about him." There are few approaches that seem to come more naturally to a student's mind than to inquire into the relation of the writer's work to his life and personality. It is a natural human concern if we are interested in a man's work to wonder what particular qualities stand behind his work.

But what are the possibilities of the expressive approach, which inquires into the way in which the work embodies some portion of the artist or ways in which a author's biography will reveal his capacity for creation? It is sometimes assumed that because the work is an expression of the writer, finding out more about the author will tell us about the work. But this is only partially true, for a literary work is not just a record of an author's life and does not necessarily reflect the events of his biography. Perhaps only the completest of diaries could achieve the kind of congruence between an author's life and work that the above quotation implies. But even a diary writer selects (consciously or unconsciously) the number of events that he records. Consequently, finding out more about the author's life would perhaps tell us what the events prior to the composition of the work were that the author chose to include or exclude, but the conclusions we would draw from those discoveries would be about him and not about the work. Students who do read about an author's life sometimes use biographical information to make statements about the relation of the work to other events in his life. This amounts to a kind of biography of the author as a person, but to say "he wrote this poem because his brother died" does not tell us much about the poem at all. It does not even tell us much about that part of the person that is a poet, for there are many people whose brothers have died that have not written poems. The "because" simply does not explain the motivation to write, nor does it explain the skill that the writer attains.

On the other hand, establishing the relationships between the events in a writer's life and works is a valuable endeavor, because when done well, it gives us knowledge about the personal context of a particular work that we did not have before. It even allows us to establish connections among various works and in doing so, gives us a sense of the writer's development. That information is valuable to us if we are interested in the writer not only as a person but also as an artist. To have a sense of the relationships of works to each other, in terms of their chronology, the place where they were written, and even the personal history of the artist at the time of composition and before allows us to gain fuller insight into the extent to which the exterior events which happen to a writer influence or do not influence his work. However, we must avoid automatically assuming that there is an influence of a biographical event on an artistic one.

Perhaps an example will help to set out more clearly the complex relationship between the events of a writer's life and his creations. In 1819, Shelley wrote "Ode to the West Wind," one of his best poems. Its subject is the power of the west wind to create new life by stripping the foliage from the trees in order to provide room for new growth and to spread the seeds for new plants. In the last two stanzas of the poem, the narrator calls upon the west wind to act on him as it acts upon the plant life to drive his own thoughts to a new birth. At the same time, however, the narrator sees himself as necessary to the west wind's creation, for only if *he* provides the seed, will the wind be able to create new life. Consequently, a union of narrator and wind is necessary for the creation of new life.

There are two fairly standard interpretations of this poem. One is that Shelley has a sense of himself as poet and prophet. His work is capable of bringing new life to men insofar as it participates in the natural power of creation symbolized and manifest in the wind. This interpretation is consistent with Shelley's own political sensitivity and his desire for political reform (if not revolution) in England. The other interpretation is that the poem is about the creation of poetry at large and that Shelley is not speaking solely of poetry that brings about political or social change, but of the power of art in general. In either case, the power, embodied in the west wind is not one that comes from the poet himself, but is something inherent in the world at large. The poet gains his own power by linking himself to that exterior power.

A study of Shelley's poetry of early 1819 supports the first interpretation. Shelley was strongly caught up in contemporary events and wrote many poems of a political nature. The most famous of those is "The Mask of Anarchy," which he wrote after hearing of the massacre at St. Peter's Fields in August of 1819. In this context, it seems likely that "Ode to the West Wind" is an expression of Shelley's desire to be the poet-prophet of the reform or revolution that will bring an end to the oppression that he earlier wrote about in "The Mask of Anarchy." This study that I have just been suggesting would be an *expressive* one which would attempt to establish the position of the "Ode" within the line of Shelley's poetic development, with specific emphasis on his ideology and his pursuit of a particular theme.

I have ignored the events of his personal life, but let me now set them out briefly: In 1816, his son William was born. His first child by Mary Shelley had died soon after birth in 1815. Between 1816 and 1819, the Shelleys traveled on the continent and in England. A daughter, who lived only a year, was born in 1817. In February of 1819, the Shelleys moved to Rome and lived there until Shelley's only son, William, died on June 7. The couple then moved to Leghorn and stayed through October (during which time Shelley composed "The Mask of Anarchy"). Mary was again pregnant, and in October, they moved to Florence, where in November, Shelley's second son was born. It was while they were in Florence that Shelley composed "Ode to the West Wind." There are two important points in this list. First, Shelley's most strongly worded political poetry was written during a time when he was not in England. In all probability, he felt physically separated from those events which he was most concerned with and wanted to be connected with them in spite of his geographical distance by envisioning himself as a prophet who could speak through the chosen word. Second is the personal note. The deaths of his children, particularly William, may have led him to think of his poetry as his progeny. The imagery of his poem entitled "To William Shelley," written in late 1819 after his son's death, is repeated in "Ode to the West Wind." That imagery affirms Shelley's faith in the natural rhythm of life as the basis for continuity, hope, and immortality, and the "Ode" says that that natural rhythm will be preserved in his "words among mankind." The cautious note of optimism at the end of the ode ("O, Wind, / If Winter comes, can Spring be far behind?") and the fact that he added the gloriously optimistic fourth act to *Prometheus Unbound* during the last months of 1819 may suggest that the anticipated birth of his next child offered him a source of hope.

This brief study does not try to account for all the poetry that Shelley wrote during 1819 nor does it even try to take into consideration the possible influence of Byron during that time, but I hope it will show how much of an awareness of a literary work and its creator one can gain from an expressive approach. I believe that it enriches our vision of a work to realize the human circumstances, whether intellectual, social, political, or personal, that are the context of its creation. But the danger is, as in all approaches, one of oversimplifying. To say that a literary work is a consequence of an event or even a series of events which we can document is to lose sight of the ultimate mystery of literary creation. For instance, regardless of what we know of the circumstances surrounding the creation of "Ode to the West Wind," we still cannot explain what led Shelley to transform those circumstances and influences into a poem, with its rich imagery, its remarkable stanza structure, and its overall form and beauty.

Another aspect of the expressive realm has to do with those parts of the artist that we do not know and which biographical facts do not explain. It is when we are dealing with that personal unknown that psychological criticism provides another approach. The study of the events in a writer's life and their relationship to his work can be called critical biography. It usually concerns itself with the events that can be documented or surmised from documentation, just as I have concerned myself with the connection between Shelley's poems and the deaths and births of his children. However, psychoanalytical criticism can be said to have grown out of a curiosity about that part of a writer's life that is not documented or is not overt in his work. The validity of the psychoanalytical approach is founded on the assumption that what is in a literary work is not only conscious expression but also unconscious expression. Or to put it another way, even if the writer does not write a poem about the death of his brother or some other event, and even if he does not wish to reveal it, we may find some evidence in his poems that those events have affected him. This possibility is based upon the notion contained in the critical adage: "The style is the man." In fuller form, the aphorism means that how a man expresses himself reveals his true personality. Thus we may find stylistic evidence in a supposedly optimistic poem that the author has a profound pessimism or a deep sense of guilt. For instance, there may be two ways of reading some poems written in the mid-1800s. There is a "public" level, in which the poems offer an optimistic moral statement. But there is also a "private" level, which reveals a sense of doubt and despair.

The heavy liability imposed on psychoanalytical criticism at the present seems to be that many readers who employ it do so without knowing what the nature of their inquiry is and what kinds of insight it can afford. Therefore, it is helpful to go back to Freud's comment on the relation of artist, work, and audience:

In the first place, [the artist] understands how to work over his daydreams in such a way as to make them lose what is too personal about them and repels strangers, and to make it possible for others to share in the enjoyment of them. He understands, too, how to tone them down so that they do not easily betray their origin from proscribed sources. Furthermore he possesses the mysterious power of shaping some particular material until it has become a faithful image of his phantasy; and he knows, moreover, how to link so large a yield of pleasure to this representation of his unconscious phantasy that, for the time being at least, repressions are out-weighed and lifted by it. If he is able to accomplish all this, he makes it possible for other people once more to derive consolation and alleviation from their own sources of pleasure in their uncon-scious which have become inaccessible to them; he earns their gratitude and admiration and he has thus achieved *through* his phantasy what originally he had achieved only *in* his phantasy—honour, power and the love of women.[8]

Freud's comment demonstrates how important the mimetic and the affective possibilities are to his definition of the art-ist's unconscious power. He says there is a quality that all people share, including the artist and the audience; it is their "human nature," their unconscious. He assumes that the un-conscious is the basis for human behavior and that it resides in all men. He bases the effect of the art on the pleasure the audience experiences from an embodiment of unconscious material and relies heavily on a notion that the basic function of art is to please rather than to instruct.

Freud also implies that there is a dual level in art that is analogous to the conscious-unconscious dualism in persons. He says that the artist reshapes his daydreams in such a way that they lose their "too personal" note. We might see this as an attempt to say as Aristotle said that art must be universal, but the next clause in Freud's comment suggests that the sur-face texture of a work of art is a mask to disguise the "pro-scribed sources" of art. (Perhaps it is a simplification of his statement that has produced the notions of needing to "read between the lines" and find "the hidden meaning.")

Yet another large statement in the passage is that the artist is one who cannot succeed through the normal channels of human endeavor and who must therefore seek his gratifica-tion by devious means which give others gratification. Such a suggestion is unfortunate and serves to demonstrate Freud's preoccupation with the "usefulness" of literary activity, though here the usefulness is to the artist rather than to his audience.

But in spite of all this theorizing about the mimetic, affective, and expressive qualities, Freud still recognizes that there is something in the artistic process that his theory does not account for. He tells us that the artist "understands how to work over his daydreams," he "tones them down," he "possesses the mysterious power of shaping some particular material . . ." There are skills that Freud acknowledges in the artist, skills which Freud's theory about the affective power can predict the outcome of, but which it does not explain. We too often forget that Freud's own statement about the psychoanalytical approach offers us knowledge about the poet and the audience as humans having a common nature, but not about what it is that makes the person into the artist. In fact, that is the danger of expressive criticism; in its valuable attempt to ascertain the relationship of the work to the artist, it may forget that the work and its maker are two different entities, and in doing so neglect the *craft*, the discipline and labor that goes into the creation of any work of art.

Though Freud did not offer a comprehensive *literary* theory, nevertheless, the method of psychoanalysis which relies on the patient's verbal expression to diagnose his unconscious lends itself easily to the critical theory that the chief source of psychoanalytical evidence is in imagery, for the imagery is part of the style, and a reflection of the way a writer inherently looks at his experience. Usually the images group themselves under a few main themes—some of the more well-known are rejection of the paternal authority, assertion of one's own sexual power (or the absence thereof), attraction to the sexual organs of the opposite sex, and attraction to the mother figure.

Perhaps the epitome of early psychoanalytical interpre-

tation is Ernest Jones's study of *Hamlet*, which expanded
Freud's notion that Hamlet was inhibited by a repressed hatred
of his father and a corresponding attraction for his mother.
Jones subsequently added to this the statement that there is a
homosexual motif in the play also, part of his evidence being
that the ear, into which Claudius poured poison, was "an unconscious equivalent for the anus" and that Claudius's attack
on his brother was "a homosexual assault." [9] Thus we may see
the way in which an image or an object can signify other
meanings through analysis of it as an image and not a mere
object.

Jones helps us make an important distinction between two
directions of psychoanalytic criticism. The comments I have
cited above are the results of his analysis of a character in the
drama, and as such, his study deals with possible *literary* aspects of *Hamlet* because it concerns itself with the motivation
of characters and the significance of their actions. But there
is another direction for psychoanalytic criticism, and that is
the use of the work to analyze the writer, which Jones goes
on to do. He says that both *Hamlet* and Shakespeare's sonnets
deal with the poet's attempts to come to terms with his own
homosexual feelings. At this point Jones is engaged in the
expressive approach that reads back through the writer's work
into the writer's life as a psychoanalyst would use a patient's
narrative or the report of a dream to analyze the patient.

The separation of the analysis of the character and its creator can be made rather easily in the case of drama and fiction;
however, there are literary works in which there seems to be
little or no separation between the artist and the material he
creates and in which, therefore, the psychoanalysis of the
work leads directly to that of the writer. This is particularly
true of poems in which the narrator of the poem speaks in the
first person and there seems to be no attempt to develop a character for that narrative voice. This persona, not a character,
but still a personage who speaks with a distinct voice, seems

to be the author. Thus, what we discover of the persona is what we discover of the writer. For example, there is a poem by Wordsworth, called "Nutting," that is ostensibly about the persona's going to gather nuts by knocking them off the trees, but the imagery of the poem is such that the nut-gathering takes on the suggestion of a sexual assault. May we presume that the persona is Wordsworth and that the poem is revelatory of his relation to the opposite sex? That is a question that we can answer only by examining other aspects of the poem and Wordsworth's poems in general. The first possible answer would be yes, because many of Wordsworth's poems are about his relationship with the natural world and he speaks of that relationship in terms of love and affection. This could lead us to develop a thesis about Wordsworth's transfer of his sexual love, for reasons unknown, from women to the natural world. However this thesis oversimplifies the content and form of Wordsworth's poems. It is also true that Wordsworth's personae are sometimes quite consciously characters, even though they are the characterizations of poets, as in "Peter Bell," or "The Idiot Boy." He is also capable of inventing characters of deranged women and old men and allowing them to speak for themselves. Therefore, it is possible that the persona in "Nutting," regardless of its similarity to Wordsworth, is another character that the poet is examining.

But there are poems with no first-person narrators that also present problems for psychoanalytic criticism. Keats's "Eve of St. Agnes" is, at the literal level, a narrative about a successful Romeo and Juliet and seems to affirm the victory of sexually consummated spiritual love over the snobbery and enmity of the social world of the lovers. Though Keats himself does not enter the poem, we can attempt to assess his relation to the subject matter by saying that Porphyro's attainment of Madeline may be Keats's wish-fulfillment of his own thwarted love for Fanny Brawne. That would be a psychoanalytical reading from poem to poet and it is a popular method. On the other hand, we may develop a psychoanalytical reading that attempts to define the affective power of the poem by demonstrating the source of the poem in what Freud called "proscribed sources." Madeline's bedchamber is the female sex organ and Porphyro is the male organ. Thus, the entire poem is about a successful sex act and gains its affective power through an appeal to the reader's subconscious desire for sexual satisfaction.

The first of the above readings may tell us something about Keats and his motivation for writing about the events that he did (although it does not tell us why he wrote a *poem*). The second interpretation tells us something about the archetypal structure and appeal of the poem. But there are many literary works and forms that contain the same basic patterns. Neither interpretation tells us much about the uniqueness and thus the *literary* value of the poem. Again, we must see that psychoanalysis can lead us away from the work itself into concerns for the artist's own subconscious or into a concern for the affective value of the work. However, some critics do concern themselves specifically with the question of the effect of the artist's personality on the work. A lucid book taking this approach is Norman Holland's *Poems in Persons*, which examines the records of H.D.'s (Hilda Doolittle) psychoanalysis under Freud in order to discover the sources of the form and content of her poems.[10] Holland's book also demonstrates how psychoanalytic technique can illuminate a reader's response to a poem. His discussions are valuable because he is careful to distinguish the limitations and possibilities of his approaches.

Psychoanalytical criticism is also valuable because it has shown us that there is a coherence in a work although it seems on the surface disordered or unclearly motivated. I have usually found it most helpful when other kinds of inquiry into a work do not yield a clear or coherent picture of it. The best example of this use of psychoanalytical criticism is also one of the best critical essays I have read. Leon Edel's chapter "Psycho-Analysis" in his *Literary Biography* combines psychoanalytical criticism with many of the critical possibilities I discuss in this chapter.[11]

There is yet another approach for expressive criticism that I should like to define. This is the study that hopes to discover in the writer's work what he believes and what his moral, philosophical, or theological position is. Again, it is like the psychoanalytical approach because it attempts to use the work in order to make a statement about the man. The danger of this approach is best exemplified by the mistake that moralists of a low order make in citing the famous speech in *Hamlet:* "Neither a borrower nor a lender be . . ." I have heard this cited as a moral dictum which Shakespeare himself approved of. Yet the source of these lines is not Hamlet, whom we might trust, or even Claudius, Hamlet's worthy foe, but the devious counsellor, Polonius. The words belong to only one of Shakespeare's characters and we would not want to make them part of the playwright's set of values. The advice may be only part of the dramatic form and motivated not by a moral sense but by the demands of the play.

It might be argued that what I have just said is true only of the artist who creates characters and who does not think of himself as a moral judge. Therefore, it might be easier and more valid to gauge the moral values of a lyric poet who speaks always in his own voice. For instance, Keats's odes must embody some kind of statement about his values, and John Donne's Holy Sonnets must embody his. But there are still qualifications: poems are not merely statements; they are more than statements and their other effects must also be taken into consideration. Also, poems are created at various moments of a poet's life and he may believe one thing in one poem and something else in another. In fact, T. S. Eliot once said, "The conscious problems with which [I am] concerned with in the actual writing are more those of a quasi-musical

nature, in the arrangement of metric and pattern, than a conscious exposition of ideas." [12] If what Eliot says is true about
the involvement of the poet in the *poetics* of the work, then
a poet may not "believe" in the content at all, but in the creation
of the work itself. The statement in the poem may not be the
point of the poem but merely part of the fabric of the greater
product which is the poem as a whole. One additional reserva-
tion about using the poems to define a poet's moral position is
that a poet does not always *know* what he is writing. He may
simply not be aware of the moral implication of a statement
that he has made, an image he has created, or a form that he has
employed or constructed.

The above expressive possibilities all depend upon separat-
ing the artist from his work, and that is as it should be. They
are both entities: the artist is flesh, blood, bone, and sinew;
the work is ink and paper, or stone, or paint. Sometimes the
approach is to bridge those entities and to see how the artist
puts himself into the work, that is, how the personality gives
form to its product, *or* how the work reveals the personality
of the artist. But an expressive approach must also admit that
the relationship of the artist to the work is a dynamic one. The
path between the artist and the work permits two-way travel.
I can best explain this by a brief history of the image of the
artist.

In the late eighteenth and early nineteenth centuries there
were a number of critics and poets writing about art that
used the analogy of the plant to describe the creative process.
Coleridge, whose statements to that effect are perhaps the best
known, said: "No man was ever yet a great poet, without being at the same time a profound philosopher. For poetry is the
blossom and the fragrancy of all human knowledge, human
thoughts, human passions, emotions, language." [13] The artist is
likened to a plant, the blossoms of which become his works.
It is a valuable analogy, for it affirms the necessity of an in-

dividual, internal unity and a vital connection between a person and his work. But the analogy has its limitations, especially at the blossom end. The creation of a work and the existence of a work often changes the artist himself. Or to be consistent with the plant analogy, not only does the blossom produce seeds which grow in new soil, but it also allows the tree itself to put out new branches and to produce still more blossoms. At one level this can be seen in the way in which artists respond to their successes and failures. On the most mundane levels, popular novelists, when they find their "formula" tend to pursue it rather than trying something else. The converse is true of their failures. At a more esthetically satisfactory level, one can see in Keats's later poetry a repetition of themes and devices that he developed in his early "Endymion" and also a preoccupation with the notion of artistic development that he evolved in some of his early verse letters as well as in "Sleep and Poetry." Artists are changed by what they create and the discoveries that they formalize in their work. Once they discover that they are able to construct a combination of devices, techniques, material, which did not have prior existence, the knowledge of that achievement, as well as the meaning of that new work, may in turn change them.

Expressive criticism, especially psychoanalytical criticism, is valuable because it teaches us that there is more to art than a conscious use of conscious materials. It teaches us that art also contains unconscious material and unconscious devices and thereby shows us that art is a rich manifestation of a human personality. But unless an expressive theory embraces a dynamic relationship between the artist and his work and admits that the dualism of the conscious-unconscious is not the total explanation of personality, and therefore of artistic creation, then it omits the single most important aspect of the artist's personality, which is neither his conscious life or his unconscious one (we all have those, artists or no), but his power to create work which is separate from him, which has an integrity of its own, and is thus capable of influencing its creator.

No study of art that omits that possibility is a study of art. It is a study of history, biography, personality, and psychology, but not of that which is the source of the value of the study of an artist's life, his work.

I have saved what I think to be the most important consideration to be made in the expressive approach until last. We must remember that the reason we return to study artists from the past is that they are not merely cultural beings who expressed an idea. If they were only that, they would not be unique. Writers of imaginative literature are not only people; they are poets, novelists, short-story writers, dramatists. They are craftsmen, and because they are, they are unique. Thus, when we choose the expressive approach and begin to inquire into the writer himself, we must always keep before us the fact that more important than our discovery of how he thought, how many wives or children he had (or abandoned), how he lived and died, is the concern of how he came to be the artist and what being an artist was for him. It has been said that there is a history of art that is separate from the history of events. It can also be said that there is a history of a person as an artist that is separate from his history as a person. John Ciardi began a recent essay on the late Louise Bogan by saying:

A poet has no true biography outside his poems. What is visible to a biographer is a physical body occupying space. At times the poet within that physical body moves, always in ways invisible to the biographer, . . . and takes on the new non-spatial existence of a poem, a kind of existence apart from the biographical "is" and into a formal "as-if."

When that motion into the "as-if" succeeds, a voice is formed, a voice always deeply related to the speaking voice of the physical identity of the poet, but always at a depth that eludes our best guesswork. When the poem is good, we have the power of its voice along with the mystery of that power.[14]

I said earlier that the task of criticism is sometimes the search for the answers to the questions "What is a poem?" "What is a play?" "What is a novel?" If our concern is not with the work, but its maker, then our questions are "What is a poet?" "What is a playwright?" "What is a novelist?" Some writers, including Coleridge and Yeats have wanted to see the writer and his work as inseparable parts. Coleridge says in his *Biographia Literaria:* "What is poetry? is so nearly the same question with, what is a poet? that the answer to the one is involved in the solution to the other. The poet, described in *ideal* perfection, brings the whole soul of man into activity, with the subordination of its faculties to each other, according to their relative worth and dignity." This then is also what a poem does. And Yeats, in the last stanza of "Among School Children" uses a metaphor from nature to describe the union of the artist with his work:

> Labour is blossoming or dancing where
> The body is not bruised to pleasure soul,
> . . . . . .
> O chestnut-tree, great-rooted blossomer,
> Are you the leaf, the blossom or the bole?
> O body swayed to music, O brightening glance,
> How can we know the dancer from the dance? [15]

What Ciardi, Coleridge, and Yeats are all speaking of is the mystery of the relation of the poem to the poet. We can continue to pursue the artist, hoping to learn what made him one, but we must not necessarily expect *the* answer. The function of criticism is not to "get to the bottom of things." That will result in reductive criticism and simplification. The true task of criticism is to illumine the mystery so that all may see it.

CHAPTER THREE

Where Do We Start?

The answer to the question "Where Do We Start?" is with the work itself. There is no other place to begin, and no good critic assumes that we read what he says before we read the work he has written about. Though I desire always to be able to use any of the approaches I have discussed in this book, my bias requires beginning with the work itself. One must always begin by finding out what the work is saying, for the critic is not responsible just to his own mind and imagination, but to the mind of the work he has chosen to study. He has a difficult task; he must maintain a balance between preserving the integrity of the work he is studying and building the integrity of his own ideas in the context of that work. If he abandons the work, he moves into the area of personal subjectivity. He may then produce a personal essay, but it will not be about the literary work in front of him. If he moves to the other extreme, he will be reduced to paraphrase and summary, and sacrifice the possibility of his new vision of the work to a mere repetition of its contents.

How does the act of making literary judgments enter into the critical process? The judgment of the quality of the work is one that can be separated from the realm of the four critical approaches and because those discussions can be only descriptive, they do not need to be accompanied by an assessment of quality. But a reader often makes implicit judgments in the way that he presents his insight and should be conscious of those judgments. The reader may decide that the work does or does not reflect some set of values which he thinks it should reflect. He may say that the work is unrealistic. These are judgments of the mimetic possibilities of the work. He may decide that the work does not have the power to give pleasure or even to create emotion in the reader. Or he may decide that it does not have the capacity to bring about action on the part of a large group of readers and thus bring about some kind of public change or reform. He may even decide that the emotional appeal of the work is wrong because of its appeal to prejudice or because of its dangerous effects and may decide that the work is only propaganda. These are all judgments of the work's effect. He may decide that the work is not a real reflection of the artist's personality and that it is inferior because it does not have the revelatory capacity he prefers. He may even decide that he does not like the personality that the work reveals. These are judgments of the expressive possibilities. He may also decide that the work is lacking in continuity, coherence, or unity, that it does not use its devices well, that the style is weak, that there are inappropriate words or contradictory ideas, or that there are clichés and trite phrases. These are judgments of the work itself, of its craft.

It is important for the reader who makes such judgments of the work itself to realize that at the base of these opinions may lie another response, his emotional one. His personal response to the poem is probably what has led him to inquire into the work itself and to consider the parts responsible for its effects. Unless the reader has a set of standards that he dispassionately applies to all works regardless of his emotions about the works, then his use of criteria of form will be born out of an attempt to discover the source of his response to an individual poem. From my own experience, it seems impossible and even wrong to maintain that dispassion. If I like a work, I shall probably become involved in trying to articulate the source of that response. If I dislike a work, I shall discover much about the work and my own tastes if I try to discover the source of that dislike.

Occasionally I make specific judgments, especially about clichés and awkward phrases. Yet as soon as I am aware of such a decision, I am uneasy. Too often, I have more or less discarded a work only to discover through a colleague's or student's comment, or through a critical essay, that I had not seen all the possibilities of that work. Then I know that I did not give the work or my insight the time or the effort to be all they could possibly be. Not long ago, I thought that I had discovered an extraneous line in Keats's "Eve of St. Agnes," until a student pointed out that it was the first hint of a theme that plays a large role in the poem.

As long as the reader is willing to change his mind and revoke or modify his own past judgments, those judgments can be of value even if they prove unsatisfactory. If they are consciously formulated, they serve as historical points in one's intellectual life, and provide at the very least a sounding board for comparing other judgments, and also a firm basis for new judgments. They are fixed points in one's thinking that can always be used as points of reference for new directions and new insights. He who uses those judgments for anything less, to build walls to defend himself against other experiences, against change, or against development, has denied himself what experience, both literary and nonliterary, can offer.

At this point, we need to make some further distinctions about a reader's attitude toward what he reads. Here W. H.

Auden can help us. He says: "If I think a form beautiful and you think it ugly, we cannot both help agreeing that one of us must be wrong, whereas if I think something is sacred and you think it is profane, neither of us will dream of arguing the matter." He also says that the process of determining beauty "is social and craves agreement with other minds." [1] This is an important idea. The act of literary criticism in its twofold state—perception and communication—is a social act. As Northrup Frye affirms: "Every deliberately constructed hierarchy of values in literature known to me is based on a concealed social, moral, or intellectual analogy." Even "Rhetorical value-judgements are closely related to social values, and are usually cleared through a customs-house of moral metaphors: sincerity, economy, subtlety, simplicity, and the like." [2] That is, even those statements which seem not to have a social or moral origin nevertheless do.

The danger then of value judgments about literature is simply that they may be wrong; they can easily be hypocritical, snobbish, or full of class prejudice. On the other hand, what about purely subjective or personal responses, in which our only comment is "To me, it's sacred"? Those subjective responses can only feed on themselves for so long before they starve, or become sterile from inbreeding. The act of reading and the study of literature is one of going outside oneself. If criticism is a twofold process—not only the expression of an individual viewpoint (which is the subjective) but also a communication of it, then criticism does exist in a realm of social values because it exists in the community of man. The reader has already moved outside himself when he reads; he may discover an even larger realm of experience and insight by comparing his judgment of what he reads to that of someone else.

The word *acceptance* is the word that my approach begins with. I cannot offer any judgment of a work (if that is my intention) until I have seen the work as fairly as possible, and that demands from me an acceptance of the work as it is. This is why I believe that Coleridge's statement about "the willing suspension of disbelief" has a wider value than its application to supernatural poetry. We must suspend our own disbelief and accept a work for what it is and does. Thus for me, the first part of critical inquiry is description in the hope of achieving a sense of what there is in a literary work. If I find that it is not "unified," whatever I choose to mean by the term, my next response is not, that it is bad or ugly or a failure, but the questions Why? and How? I find that I do not often judge the quality of the work as a result of this analysis. By the time I have finished my own process of discovery about the work, the work is too much a part of my own intellectual history for me to make such a detached response. If the work has contributed to my insight, then I must recognize that it has had value to me even if I find it lacking in technique or logic or what have you.

The essential quality of the student of literature is a wholly flexible response. He must be willing always to put aside the predisposition of his morality and of his previous literary experience, and take up a new work with as much innocence as he can muster. Only then can he give the work what it deserves, his entire attention and a willingness to accept it for what it is. Then, after that, he may pursue his own areas of inquiry which may be questions about the form or shape of the work and the interrelationships of its various parts, questions about its relationship to its creator, its effect on its own time and its possible effect on readers now, or he may wish to inquire into the nature of the truth of the work and the extent to which it reflects its age or the permanent qualities of all time.

Then the student must try to convey as clearly and coherently as possible what his own perception of that work is. But that presentation should also contain the same passion that the student's inquiry should have. Insofar as the presentation of one reader's interpretation of a work is invested with the sense of excitement, discovery, and pleasure if not in the work, nevertheless in the process of interpretation, his vision will be significant and valuable to his audience. To the extent that the reader knows that I am describing the work as it appears on the page and to the extent that he can grasp my interpretation, not only the content but also the spirit of it— to that extent I have succeeded. He may disagree with my interpretation, but if I have given him a new way of seeing the literary work then I have done what a critic should do.

The various critical approaches are always options; nevertheless, they are *critical* options. They ask the reader to discern and define his relationship to what he has read. Just as there are teachers who do not desire to give their students a choice of possibilities, so there are students who do not wish to go beyond their primary emotional response to the text. They do not care for literary criticism. The difference between those who do and those who don't is curiosity. Those who are willing to engage in criticism, either by reading it or by writing their own, are usually interested in the larger relationships that literature may develop and not merely in the nonverbal and unanalyzable emotional response. That is not to discount that response, for it is basic. But literature does not stay within the boundaries of any area of human experience, including the solely emotional. Once a student asks himself the smallest question about the work and seeks to answer it, he has begun a critical inquiry which only stops when he chooses to stop it. Moreover, the phrase, "critical inquiry" should not be a bugaboo, for it does not mean dissection; it means simply that the student has allowed his intellect as well as his emotions into his reading experience and the paths which his curiosity may take are manifold.

When Auden speaks of "grown-up" critics and poets, he seems to be speaking of those who feel the necessity to judge. But to come to a final judgment is to come to the end of the possibilities of the work and often to deny the possibility that the work will have further influence or reveal greater richness as the reader develops. The act of love is that of willing that which is loved to fulfill itself, and of making sure that no possibility for fulfillment is ignored. Blackmur is right when he says that criticism is like walking; it is only for one who is still moving and growing.

CHAPTER FOUR

Using the Possibilities

To conclude, I want to move the discussion from a general level to an immediate and practical one. I am going to choose a poem from a popular anthology and suggest the kinds of questions and issues that considering it under each of the four approaches can raise. There are both disadvantages and advantages to this. The disadvantage is that taking up one approach at a time in arbitrary arrangement is unnatural. The reader should begin from his point of interest and establish the relations of other aspects of the work to that central focus. (I offer my version of this more natural approach in the second half of this section.) However, there are two advantages: 1) taking up the inquiry according to the categories will allow us to see both the limitations and the overlap of questions and issues that are raised; 2) the process of choosing the poem will be similar to the way in which a student meets a reading assignment.

I choose from a popular anthology; my only stipulation is

that the poem be short enough to discuss here. I discover
Emily Dickinson's "The Clover's simple Fame": [1]

> The Clover's simple Fame
> Remembered of the Cow—
> Is better than enameled Realms
> Of notability.
> Renown perceives itself
> And that degrades the Flower—
> The Daisy that has looked behind
> Has compromised its power.

I have never seen this poem before and I know little about
Emily Dickinson, but let me see what I can discover about
the poem. It is a discussion of kinds of fame—there is the
"simple Fame" of the Clover because it is "Remembered by
the Cow;" there is "notability;" and there is "Renown." There
is also a value judgment in the poem. The Clover's fame is
preferable to "notability" and to that of the Daisy. Moreover,
the Clover seems to take precedence over a Flower, which is
degraded. But at this point I am confused. Are there three
kinds of fame: Fame, Notability, and Renown, or are the last
two the same?

What do I recognize from my world that applies to the
poem? The Cow eats the Clover and is itself not a conceptual-
izing creature; thus if the poem says that the Clover is "remembered" by the Cow (here I translate the ambiguous "of"
to mean "by"), it must mean that the Cow remembers the
Clover by making it into nourishment. Memory is not mental
then, but physical. The "simple Fame" then seems to mean a
natural life-giving process.

Now, how do I understand "Realms/ Of notability"? I recall that notability is a concept not a country, and I see that
the poem moves quickly to abstractions. But I'm still confused by the word "Renown;" it seems much like "Fame";

yet "Renown" is a negative quality in the poem and "Fame" is positive.

Then the last sentence: "The Daisy that has looked behind/ Has compromised its power" introduces a new element. The Daisy now has human characteristics; it has looked and has compromised itself.

I am at the end of the present mimetic possibilities, though I still have not answered all the questions I have about the poem, the chief one being how is the poem significant or true? I have an inkling that the poem has large moral implications because of its topic, which is fame, and because the Daisy is personified, but I do not know what they are yet.

What about the affective possibilities? Are there lines that have particular appeal? Not yet. The first effect is one of curiosity about the relationships of the parts of the poem and its statement.

Moreover, at this point I can do nothing about the expressive possibilities, for I know almost nothing about Emily Dickinson; nor do I see any reason to try a Freudian reading of the poem. I look back at the beginning of the Dickinson selections in the anthology, but the headnote gives only her birth and death dates. What I remember of the lore about her is that she was unmarried, lived alone, wore white, and perhaps had a love affair. That's no help. The expressive possibilities will have to wait until I can find out more about her life.

My real focus at this point must return to the poem for itself. Though I know nothing of the background of the poem, I do know something about the individual phrases of the poem, and that the poem is about common objects and ideas. Perhaps a study of the interrelationships between the phrases and the ideas will tell me more. I begin to see the implications of "enameled." The "Clover's simple Fame" is better because it is natural, organic, and contributes to growth. The "enameled Realms" are more than merely stiff and formal, they are, by comparison, unnatural. Now there is suddenly an added dimension to the affective possibilities of this poem, for I have discovered the quiet humor of contrasting a homely domestic animal chewing clover to the trappings of royalty. Also, I think I know why the poem uses "Of" rather than "by." The "of" means that the Cow's memory is not an isolated mental quality; the memory of the Cow is its physical being. The Clover has become part *of* the Cow's life.

The insights about this first sentence make the second clearer. I see that "notability" and "Renown" are placed next to each other in the poem and I assume that they are similar, and that assumption leads me to another level of reading. If both perceive themselves, then they both have another shortcoming besides unnaturalness; they are both self-conscious. The Clover eaten by the Cow is not, and it is therefore not degraded. I understand now that the Flower is not the Clover, but I'm still bothered by a mimetic difficulty. I think of clover as having flowers, yet the poet does not. So I try the dictionary to reassure myself. Right, it's a legume with clusters of flowers. I decide that it is the contrast between Clover and Daisy that has led the poet to call only the daisy a flower. Then on an impulse I look up "Daisy," and find out of course that it's a flower; but I also discover that its name is special. It comes from the Old English words, "day's eye." Then I realize why the poet has used the flower that is the "day's eye"; it can look back on its own life and fame and conclude that it is a beautiful object. In doing so, it compromises its "power" by being self-conscious, and is wrong about the lasting quality of its beauty.

My attention now returns to the beginning, for there is where the Clover is, the plant to be valued most, because it has not compromised its power. Instead, its being eaten by the cow has given it greater power than the beautiful flowers have gained, which possess Renown. I see also that there is an implied connection between the Daisy and the "enameled

Realms of notability," because of the similar locations of the two in their respective sentences and in the form of the poem. That connection suggests that the Daisy itself is stiff, artificial, and lifeless.

I have been through four areas of possible literary inquiry. Because of my own knowledge and lack of it (especially of the poet), not all areas have been equally available to me, and the most valuable approach has been a combination of the mimetic and a consideration of the interrelationships of the parts of the poem. At this point I can add further to the mimetic (and by implication to the affective). Though the poem is ostensibly about flowers, it suggests a human message by its use of objects from the human world, by its abstractions, and by its personification of the Daisy. Consequently, there are two levels of broader interpretation possible. The first is a commentary on "Fame" which is associated with physical beauty. There are two kinds of beauty—the artificial which is self-conscious and therefore self-degrading, and the natural and life-giving that is egoless and permanent because it sustains life. The poem makes clear which we should prefer. Is there also a message here for people? Does the poem imply something about the kind of beauty people have or the kind of fame they should seek? I think it does; the poem introduces elements from the human world, such as Fame, Realms, and self-consciousness, which have no existence in real plants.

What about the affective level of interpretation? That depends upon the immediacy of the moral statement we attach to the poem. However, I would say that its message is private rather than public. There is no call for collective action and not even any demand for change on the part of the individual. Moreover, it is not a comment on the failure of monarchial government or indicative of a preference for the "people." On the other hand, it does offer a judgment about which beauty is to be preferred; and a perception of that judgment could change a reader's concept of his or her personal goals.

What about the expressive level? That is an area I would have to give more study to, but I can suggest the kinds of questions and inquiries that could be valuable. First, I might study the poem in relation to Dickinson's artistic career. What is the position of the poem among her other poems? Is it similar in theme or form to others of the same time or to all her others? Does the poem indicate any development? Does it contain a new use of flower imagery or sound devices? What is the relation of the poem to the themes of her other poems? Are there others which make the same statements about personal values and about the qualities of beauty? Does such a message appear often enough that we could say that it seems to be one of Dickinson's beliefs or is it an idea she is trying out? Is it possible that the poem is even a statement about poems themselves—that they are to give life by being taken up by the reader and not just "enameled" decorations? We might also want to carry our inquiry into the poet's personal life instead of considering only her life as a thinker and artist. Does the poem reveal the way in which she thinks of her personal beauty or herself as a woman? These are all questions which the expressive approach would lead us to and which would add to our insight into the poem and the author.

One more inquiry: Is the poem good or bad? Earlier I said that the interest I had in the poem was primarily in discovering what it was saying. Then I found the quiet humor of the Cow's digestion being preferred to "enameled Realms." A second pleasant discovery was the pun on "day's eye" which completed the personification of the daisy. It is for me an enjoyable poem and discovering what I have has also been enjoyable. I like the poem. But what about its quality? One could judge it in terms of its unity. It is coherent in its statements and imagery, and its ability to reflect on itself and create interrelationships give it the appeal of wholeness. In those terms it is a good poem.

What about its precision of statement? The first sentence is good, for the natural opposed to the unnatural is concisely set out. I was for awhile less satisfied with the second sentence of the poem. My criterion was a sense of where the emphasis *should* be as a result of deciding that the first sentence is good. Then I saw the way in which the poem moves from the visual image of the Clover and Cow through the abstractions back to the visual image of the Daisy. Also, the phrase "has looked behind" seemed vague. I asked "looked behind what?" and answered "itself," when I thought it should be looking behind into time. Then when I found that the Daisy was a "day's eye," I realized that "itself" (the daisy) contained the element of time in the "day"!

Even as I discover that the poem is tightly knit and well-balanced, and that the discovery of those qualities in it pleases me, I realize also that no single answer to the question of quality is possible. I can still ask how significant the poem is in terms of its idea and realize that I have read many other poems that are more important. On the other hand, the more I find out about the poem, the less concerned I become with its quality. When I have studied and written or talked about a poem, it is difficult to find serious fault with it even if I know it may be a minor poem. It has become a part of my thinking, and studying it is itself a source of value.

What I intend to do next is to discuss a short poem and show that the four areas of possibilities are not necessarily to be kept separate. In the previous discussions I have separated them to demonstrate their capacities and limitations. The reason for identifying the approaches and the areas they concern is to provide for the conscious awareness of their use. However, in any natural critical endeavor, they work together to show the manifold significance of the work.

I have chosen W. B. Yeats's "On Being Asked for a War

Poem." [2] I only recently discovered it in rereading Yeats's work, and it has become important to me. I choose to write about it here because I like it.

> I think it better than in times like these
> A poet's mouth be silent, for in truth
> We have no gift to set a statesman right;
> He has had enough of meddling who can please
> A young girl in the indolence of her youth,
> Or an old man upon a winter's night.

Let me tell you why I like it.

My first discovery was that Yeats was refusing to write a war poem and that he was offering his reason for doing so. At this point I saw the poem from an affective point of view. I intended to read it to a class that felt that poets should concern themselves with the catastrophes in human history. I wanted the poem to affect them. But as I read it aloud in preparation for the class, it began to affect me. It was my sense of the relation between the sentences of the poem and their form on the page. The first line ends with a slight pause and then pushes on to complete itself gramatically:

> I think it better that in times like these
> A poet's mouth be silent,

The first line rings changes on the "i" sound to give the line a smoothness and then pushes into the second line to end with the word "silent," which repeats the "i" sound again and also ends the phrase, but only briefly. Then we are given the rest of the sentence: "for in truth/ We have no gift to set a statesman right." What I am continually excited about in this poem is the tension that Yeats generates between the push of his sentence and the containment that his strict stanza structure creates.

But the poem does not come to a full stop at the end of the

third line; it suddenly devalues setting statesmen right, which is only "meddling." It is more important to "please/ A young girl in the indolence of her youth,/ Or an old man upon a winter's night." With these lines the poem is complete not only in its statement and its grammar (the poem is only one sentence), but also in its rhyme. Now the end-words of the lines in the first half of the poem, *these*, *truth*, and *right*, are combined with the end-words in the last half, *please*, *youth*, and *night*. Even the coincidence of the words add meaning; *truth* now connects with pleasing a youth, and what will set a statesman right has been transformed into what will please an old man in a "winter's night."

But the possibilities of the form are even richer. The poem goes from what should be most important socially or historically, a poet's message to a statesman, to the apparent trivia of giving delight to young girls and old men. Yet in the middle of the poem, the message to the statesman has been renamed "meddling" and the imagery of the young girl and the old man upon a winter's night gives value to what should have been unimportant.

I do not choose here to go further into a study of the poem's metrical effect, but it would be a valuable study, because it would demonstrate to an even greater degree, how carefully Yeats manages his verbal effects. On the other hand, what I want to do is to show the further possibilities for critical inquiry. The process I have been engaged in above is an "objective" one. I have been considering the poem in and for itself, but I have also been trying to convey the effects of the poem's devices on myself and to convey my responses to it. I have done an "analysis," but it is not for the purpose of "tearing the poem apart." It is intended to convey as precisely as possible my sense of the artistry of the poem and its importance to me. That is the real point and value of "analysis;" it is the attempt to convey, by citing details and explaining their interworkings, the unnamable effect of the poem. The process is a paradox; analysis attempts not to reduce but to set up patterns which will *convey* the indefinable beauty of a work.

If I were to return to the poem I might choose a different approach. Yeats says "in times like these" and reveals a sense of the relation of his poem to the events of his own day. I discover that the poem was included in the poems he published in 1919 under the title *The Wild Swans at Coole* and that it appeared with such poems as "In Memory of Major Robert Gregory" and "An Irish Airman Foresees His Death." Another kind of knowledge I could gain about the poem would be about the events before its composition. Was there a specific person who asked Yeats to write a poem? Did Yeats and this person oppose each other in their views of the war or did they agree? Such details as these and others would be part of a "mimetic" approach to the poem. I could go on to ask how similar the events surrounding the poem then are to events today. Then perhaps I would want to make some comment about whether Yeats's poem really is an answer to those who say that the job of the poet is social protest.

Here I must digress just as my critical endeavor has. As I was leafing through the other poems of 1919, I was struck by the possibility of reading all the poems in that volume and attempting to ascertain their relationships in terms of their subjects, imagery, and styles. Moreover, there are many poems I should like to read and write on individually. For instance, "Memory."

> One had a lovely face,
> And two or three had charm,
> But charm and face were in vain
> Because the mountain grass
> Cannot but keep the form
> Where the mountain hare has lain.[3]

I would like to study and write about this poem because of the cause-effect relationship Yeats sets up between beauty and the mountain grass and the mountain hare. Here my beginning curiosity is not about the subject of the poem so much as the implications of the grammatical form.

But at no time am I far from wondering about the relation of "On Being Asked for a War Poem" to Yeats's life. When I read a number of his poems, I discover not only something about his poems, but also something about his life. And when I read about Irish history in 1919 or about his life, I know something else about the "world" of his poems.

Before long, the poem is not only a skillful verbal pattern that amazes me with its appeal, but it is also a focal point, a center around which the knowledge I have of Yeats, his time, and his other poems coalesces. The poem has become a world. And not only what I have found out for myself by textual analysis but also what I have learned from others about Yeats and his time becomes a part of my knowledge. Those "facts" which we often think of as being trivial, are now a part of a personal knowledge I have which enriches the poem and me.

This is the time now to read what others have said about the poem and about Yeats's poetry. Now I have a personal frame for others' opinions which will allow me to sort out what seems of value from what is not. And as I read, I can test my own conceptions of the poem against those of others, and find out even more clearly what I know, and need to know. I may even discover that part of what I know is what most readers know. On the other hand, what I have discovered may be something that no one else has written about. Moreover, in the dynamic process of stacking my own opinions against others, I may find that my own knowledge has grown as a result of the impetus that those other opinions have given me. Something new may occur to me that will give me an even richer sense of the poem.

The study of literature or even of an individual work ends only when the reader ceases to be interested in it; for if he continues to inquire, he will always find new insight. Moreover, if he returns to the work later, he will find that the experiences he has had between times will give him a new framework and often a new concern. The purpose of this book has not been to pursue a specific approach nor even to exhaust the possibilities of criticism. Rather, I hope that it has affirmed the humanness, even the naturalness of literary inquiry and shown the broad possibilities for study and insight available to the reader whose curiosity does not cease at the end of the last page of what he is reading.

Bibliographical Notes

CHAPTER ONE

1. "The Necessity of Art," *Saturday Review*, 6 December 1969, p. 26.
2. "Polemical Introduction," *Anatomy of Criticism* (New York: Atheneum, 1969), p. 11.
3. "A Critic's Job of Work," *The Double Agent: Essays in Craft and Elucidation* (New York: Arrow Editions, 1935), p. 277.

CHAPTER TWO

1. See Chapter one of *The Mirror and the Lamp* (New York: Oxford University Press, 1953).
2. William Blake, "The Tyger," *The Norton Anthology of English Literature*, Revised, ed. M. H. Abrams, *et al.* (New York: W. W. Norton & Co., Inc., 1968), II, 717–719. Copyright © 1968, 1962, by W. W. Norton & Co., Inc.
3. *Biographia Literaria*, Chap. XIV.
4. "Making, Knowing, and Judging," *The Dyer's Hand* (New York: Random House, 1962), p. 40.

5. "Preface," *The Nigger of the Narcissus* (New York: Doubleday, Page & Company, 1924), p. xiv.

6. *Black Magic: Poetry 1961–1967* (New York: Bobbs-Merrill Company, 1969), p. 116.

7. *The Will to Change: Poems 1968–1970* (New York: W. W. Norton & Co., Inc., 1971), p. 14.

8. *The Complete Introductory Lectures on Psychoanalysis*. Trans. and ed. James Strachey (New York: W. W. Norton & Co., Inc.), pp. 376–7.

9. "The Death of Hamlet's Father," *Essays in Psychoanalysis*. 2 vols. (London: Hogarth Press, Ltd., 1951), I, 326.

10. *Poems in Persons* by Norman Holland (New York: W. W. Norton & Co., Inc., 1973).

11. *Literary Biography* by Leon Edel (London: Rupert Hart Davis, 1957).

12. Quoted in *Poetic Meter and Poetic Form* by Paul Fussell, Jr. (New York: Random House, 1965), pp. 3–4.

13. *Biographia Literaria*, Chap. XV, sec. 4.

14. *Saturday Review*, 21 September 1970, p. 20.

15. *The Collected Poems of W. B. Yeats* (New York: The Macmillan Company, 1956), pp. 212–4. Reprinted by permission of Mr. M. B. Yeats, the Macmillan Company of Canada Ltd., and Macmillan. Copyright 1919 by Macmillan Publishing Co., Inc., renewed 1947 by Bertha Georgie Yeats.

CHAPTER THREE

1. "Making, Knowing, and Judging," *The Dyer's Hand* (New York: Random House, 1962), p. 57.

2. "Polemical Introduction," *Anatomy of Criticism* (New York: Atheneum, 1969), pp. 23 and 21.

CHAPTER FOUR

1. *The Poems of Emily Dickinson*, ed. Thomas H. Johnson (Cambridge, Mass.: Harvard University Press, 1951), #1232. Reprinted by permission of the publishers and the Trustees of Amherst College from Thomas H. Johnson, editor, *The Poems of Emily Dickinson*, Cambridge, Mass.: The Belknap Press of Harvard University Press. Copyright, 1951, 1955, by the President and Fellows of Harvard College.

2. Yeats, p. 153. Reprinted by permission of Mr. M. B. Yeats, The Macmillan Company of Canada, Ltd., and Macmillan. Copyright

1919 by Macmillan Publishing Co., Inc., renewed 1947 by Bertha Georgie Yeats.

3. Yeats, p. 147. Reprinted by permission of Mr. M. B. Yeats, The Macmillan Company of Canada Ltd., and Macmillan. Copyright 1919 by Macmillan Publishing Co., Inc., renewed 1947 by Bertha Georgie Yeats.